ACTA UNIVERSITATIS UPSALIENSIS
Studia Doctrinae Christianae Upsaliensia
21

LiberTryck Stockholm 1981   123174

Anna-Stina Ellverson

The Dual Nature of Man
A Study in the Theological Anthropology of Gregory of Nazianzus

UPPSALA 1981

Distributors:

Almqvist & Wiksell International

Stockholm — Sweden

Doctoral Thesis at Uppsala University 1981

ISBN 91-554-1206-8
ISSN 0585-508X

BR
65
.G76
E44
1981

Ellverson, A.: The Dual Nature of Man. A Study in the Theological Anthropology of Gregory of Nazianzus. *Studia Doctrinae Christianae Upsaliensia* 21, 119 pp. Uppsala 1981. ISBN 91-554-1206-8. ISSN 0585-508X.

Abstract
This study deals with some aspects of the anthropology of Gregory of Nazianzus (fourth century), one of the so called Cappadocian Fathers. For Gregory man was a double or compounded being, made up of spirit and matter or body and soul. This doubleness, with its two aspects of man is an important part of his theology.

In the first part of the study, in chapter 2, which is of a more descriptive character, Gregory's view on man as a spiritual and bodily being is covered as well as his understanding of man as a "mixed" and composed being. Further the double nature of man causes questions and reflections, which concern a more existential aspect of life. In chapter 3, under the heading "Why is man a bodily being", some texts and passages are presented in which Gregory more or less directly poses the question concerning the reasons for man's bodily and double nature. Here we find reflections on the significance of man's bodily life and implicitly even of his life on earth. In this chapter also basic aspects are dealt with which concern the existence of man, such as freedom, his original weakness and the necessity of making decision concerning good and the life with God. In reading the theology of Gregory it is further possible to discern what may be called a theological system in which man as a double being of spirit and matter forms a part. In chapter 4, this system is presented and some structures or patterns are discussed, which characterize it. Some aspects of the relation of man and creation to the Trinity are dealt with in the last chapter. Even the Father and the Spirit have a relation to man and creation. If this is not observed we risk an understanding of Gregory which is too exclusively Christocentric.

A. Ellverson, Faculty of Theology, Box 2006, S-750 02 Uppsala, Sweden.

Printed in Sweden by
LiberTryck, Stockholm 1981

Phototype setting by
Textgruppen i Uppsala AB

Contents

Chapter 1
Introduction

1. The contribution of the Cappadocian theology

In general literature on the early Christian period and its theology, the three Cappadocian theologians from the later part of the fourth century, Basil of Caesarea, his friend Gregory of Nazianzus and the younger brother of Basil, Gregory of Nyssa, mainly are known for their contribution in the field of Trinitarian theology and Christology.[1] We are here confronted with a theological work on the basis of the creed from the council of 325 and the heritage of Athanasius, as well as from the older Alexandrian theology.

In the fields of anthropology and cosmology, their teaching and contribution is less well known, and in the common literature on this period is generally just hinted at or not observed. The anthropology of Gregory of Nyssa though, who is regarded of the three as the one who most thoroughly has worked with the question of man, is the object of a certain number of studies.[2]

The teaching on man and creation of the Cappadocian Fathers is less easily discerned and understood in the context of the early Christian period than is the case with their Trinitarian theology and Christology. This fact is owed to a lack of general works or surveys on patristic teaching on man and creation or attempts to summarize what has so far been done in this theological field.[3]

2. Man and creation. A third line of thought during the patristic period

From the systematic point of view Trinitarian theology and Christology generally are presented as the main lines of thought during the patristic period. Without denying the dominance of these two issues, I think that, as a third line of thought during this period, we should regard the thinking and reflection on man and creation, their relationship to God (as well as to each other) and the questions concerning the existence of man and the significance of his life.

Now the main purpose of this study is not an attempt to sketch such a line of thought or to characterize the thinking of Gregory of Nazianzus in relation to it, though in some respects, I think we are right to regard the thinking of Gregory as a link in such a train of thought. Perhaps we may say that certain ideas, as well as problems or questions, are formulated by some theologians, inherited and adapted by others, worked upon and sometimes used in a different way together with new or differently understood problems and questions and in their turn passed on to others. So I think it in some respects is possible to see and understand the thinking of Gregory of Nazianzus on man as well on creation as a link of such a line, to which we among others may count Irenaeus of Lyon, the Alexandrian theologians, Clement and Origen as well as the later Father, Maximus the Confessor.[4]

What concerns the understanding of man the Cappadocians in general may be said to belong to a tradition for which it was essential to stress the creation of man as an *image of God* and *theosis* or divinisation as his final goal. The *double nature of man* as a being composed of both body and soul or matter and spirit and a more or less dualistic[5] view of this union is another characteristic feature. A further dominant feature in this tradition of man and his existence is the underlining of the *freedom of man* and, according to the teaching of many of the theologians, the understanding of the primordial, original man as a "child" or a *yet not perfect being* (among the Cappadocians this latter idea was held by Basil and Gregory of Nazianzus).[6] All these ideas of man are found in the theology of Gregory and we shall see the way they form a part of his theology.

3. Certain underlying questions and problems

From one point of view I think it is possible to understand the early Christian thinking on man and creation as a dealing with and a work upon certain questions, more or less articulated, and as an attempt to give an answer to these questions. In the study of different theologians, I would further propose that it is possible to work on different "levels". So in the study of their view of man, it is possible to try to recapitulate different ideas and give an account of their thinking in different respects in a merely descriptive way. We may thus try to find out their understanding in different respects and for example describe their ideas about man as an "image" of God or about "theosis" or divinisation. We may try to give an account for how they describe and understand the original, primordial man, or man's bodily nature respectively before and after the fall or other "parts" of their anthropology. Now this is quite necessarily a work which has to be done and which has its own value and importance. But, in a way, it is a rather "technical" way of looking at and studying the subject which might be supplemented by an attempt to a study on a somewhat deeper level. What I mean is that this more descriptive way of working should, or at least could be complemented with a search for and a discussion of the underlying questions and problems which may be found in the thinking of a certain theologian or in a whole period, either as pronounced problems or underlying unarticulated questions.

Now this kind of work has got a greater amount of uncertainty and thus a more hypothetical character than the more technical and descriptive method referred to above. I think it is possible though, to a certain degree, to understand at least some of the reflections and ideas about man during the patristic period, as caused by certain problems and as a result of reflection which was dictated by certain questions concerning the existence of man and his life. So I think that in the study of the anthropology of the early Christian period not only should we not stop at the mere descriptive and technical level consisting of a description of their ideas about man as an "image" of God, as a "free" being, etc. but try to go one step further and look for the underlying questions or problems.

One reason for this is the fact that among these underlying questions we find problems with which man has always been confronted and for which he has searched for answers. If this is true, this means that we have, in the patristic period, important reflections and ideas which have reference to and concern our own questions and thinking.

Some of their questions Christians shared with their non-Christian contemporaries and the theologian's task here was to find an answer that coincided with Christian tradition and belief. Such a question for example was the problem of evil or the darker and negative aspect of life and its origin and nature. This question I for example think might be regarded as a question which contributed to Irenaeus understanding of the primordial man as a free being but also as "childish" and not yet perfect.[7]

Another question with which I think we are either indirectly or explicitly confronted during this period is a question caused by the strongly dualistic view of man.[8] This question might be formulated as the search for or question of the reasons for man's earthly life and for his bodily life and the significance of it. Or perhaps we rather should say the present, actual kind of bodily life. Why should man live this life on earth? What has caused it or what are the reasons for it?

So the theology of Origen with his famous idea about the prehistoric fall before the creation of this material, earthly world might be understood as an attempt to give reason for the actual life on earth. Why do we live this life? Man is here because he has suffered a fall in a previous existence and now this world and this life are the circumstances of his "return" to God and for the pedagogical chastement, correction and salvation of man by God.[9]

In the thinking of the two Gregories we find a similar question dealt with in different ways. Gregory of Nyssa: If man is the great being created into the image and likeness of God, how could this fact be conciliated with the miserable, deathly and bodily existence of man?[10] Or as we will reconstruct the question of Gregory of Nazianzus (though he himself never expresses the question in this form): If man is a spiritual being created for a spiritual life with God in the heavenly existence, why should he then live this kind of hard and troublesome life on earth?

4. A Platonizing theology

Gregory of Nazianzus together with the two other Cappadocian theologians belongs to those of the fathers who generally are characterized as "Platonizing" and they here in many respects are the heirs of the heritage of the older Alexandrian theology (Clement, Origen).

We are here confronted with a Hellenistic or Platonic[11] form of Christianity which with regard to the anthropology means a particular dualistic view of man as a double natured being of spirit and matter, a stressing of the spiritual aspect and a corresponding less positive attitude to the bodily one.

The particular "Platonism" or "Hellenism" of Gregory is observed and dealt with in some other studies of him[12] and shall not be the object of this study. Yet a remark should be made here which concerns the understanding of the authors about the relation between the Platonism and the Christian belief in the thinking of Gregory. In the studies here referred to the Hellenism or Platonism of Gregory is stated and sometimes discussed in very informative detail. At the same time though the integrity of Gregory's authentically Christian belief is stated and vindicated. Where it concerns the relationship between the Platonic and the Christian elements, the authors generally speak about an association between Platonism and Christian belief. Thus the latter, the Christian belief, is understood as to have the final word and the Platonism is understood as having the rank of a helpmate.[13] The integrity of the Christian belief in this association is thus vindicated. As a background for this judgment I think we are right to see an older, more negative attitude to the "Hellenism" of the early church as causing a change to a less authentic form of Christian belief.[14] The authors are eager to stress the integrity of the Christian faith in its encounter with Greek culture.

This opinion of those authors shall not be questioned here (and I am sure their judgment in general corresponds to the conscious attitude of Gregory himself), but what I miss in this literature is a pursuing of the question one step further, namely to a discussion of what this association meant for Christian faith and tradition. Do we not here very clearly have a particular type of Christianity with a particular outlook, and a particular perspective, and stress on certain elements while others are moved in the background? This question is not dealt with in the literature referred to above.

The whole issue is observed though by R. Ruether in her study on Gregory of Nazianzus and she remarking upon it—in this case though referring to the other two Cappadocians—states, "In their hands the fusion of Christianity with monasticism and Platonic spirituality becomes complete. For them it is axiomatic to describe Christianity in terms of monastic life, and, in turn, to describe monastic life in a language derived from Alexandrian Platonism. Thus by their time, the equation of Christian with monk was widely accepted."[15]

5. The theme of the study

5.a. The double nature of man

For Gregory the doubleness of man as a composed being of body and soul or matter and spirit has got a basic role for his theology and thinking. In his understanding of reality we find two, or rather three kinds of natures or spheres, first God, and then the created spheres, spirit and matter. Man, thanks to his double nature, has got a kind of middle position belonging both to the spiritual sphere and the material and earthly one. So Gregory in one of his orations is saying, "I am small and great, lowly and high, mortal and immortal, earthly and heavenly. The one condition I share with this world below, the other with God, the one with the flesh, the other with the spirit."[16]

In the theology of Gregory we, systematically speaking, find two sides, which both will be discussed in this study and which might be characterized as a more existential perspective and, a more ontological one. For both these sides of his thinking the doubleness of man has got an important role.

1) First it awakes and causes certain questions and reflections of an existential and personal kind more or less articulated as the following. Why this doubleness? Why this kind of body? Or, as the question already has been formulated, if man is to live a spiritual life in the heavenly existence, why this kind of troublesome, bodily life? Over these questions Gregory has considerable reflections and answers which concern the significance of the life of man and basic datas of his existence.

2) The dichotomy of the nature of man forms and constitutes an important and crucial role of what we may call the theological or ontological system of Gregory also. Further these two sides, the existential and the ontological, might be seen as two sides or aspects of the same story, namely, the creation of the world by God, his giving of existence to it as well as its way to him in which the way of man and his destiny as a free being and as a being created for a life with God plays an important role.

5.b. The opposite perspective

Seen from our own contemporary, western point of view the Platonic perspective of Gregory on man is the opposite to the perspective of our own time. We may say that for Gregory the spiritual aspect of life was not only the dominant one but even the most self evident one, never questioned as such.

That which caused the questions was rather the bodily, material aspect of life. For our culture and our time the perspective is the reverse. The bodily or the biological, physical aspect of life is the self evident one, while the spiritual is not and is even questioned as to its own existence.

That which is not self evident now is what actually raises the questions and accordingly may cause reflections. So we find in the thinking of Gregory,

13

thanks to his different, opposite perspective another type of questions and reflections than those we generally make, concerning the meaning and significance of the earthly life of man. In the texts[17] where these ideas of Gregory are developed we find reflections which in their literal expression or in their consequences deeply concern the existence of man. We may or we may not share the perspective of Gregory but nevertheless I think it is right to claim the great value and interest of these texts.

5.c. Content of the study

In the first part of this study, Chapter 2, which has a more descriptive character Gregory's view on man as a spiritual and bodily being is covered as well as his understanding of man as a "mixed" and composed being.

The second part, Chapter 3, mainly deals with the more existential aspect of his anthropology. Under the head line of "Why is man a bodily being" some main texts and passages are presented in which Gregory more or less directly poses the question concerning the reasons for man's bodily and double nature or on the whole gives an account of man's composition as both a bodily and spiritual being. Doing this he presents us with the ideas and reflections referred to in the passage above (section 5.b.), and the study of these ideas invites us to work with Gregory's understanding of the basic data of the life and existence of man. Here we find his understanding of the first, "new created", primordial man as well as his ideas about the fall or lapse of man. In order to understand the texts it has been necessary to deal rather exhaustively with these two latter issues, Gregory's idea about the primal man, Adam and his tendency to a fall as well as the lapse as such.

Further, in the theology of Gregory, something that may be called a theological system is found, though Gregory himself generally does not speak in terms of a system or present us with any. Nevertheless, if we go through his thinking about God, creation, man, incarnation and the final theosis and restoration something comparable to a system becomes discernable. This system is first treated in chapter 4, and presented so that we may reconstruct it. Some characteristic features and patterns of it are discussed. In that chapter an attempt is also made to discuss the relationship of Gregory to the Platonic or Platonizing tradition, what concerns his theological system and ontology. In this respect Gregory is both understood as belonging to the Platonic tradition as well as breaking with it.

The last part of the study, chapter 5, deals with the relation of man and creation to the Trinity in some different respects.

It should so be said, especially in chapter 3 and 5, that beside the interpretation and discussion of what Gregory more directly and explicitly is saying in the texts, there is also an attempt made to go one step further at some points. I have thus tried to show some possible ways of interpretations for which the texts are open and further attempted to show what might be understood as implied in Gregory's thinking, though not explicitly expressed, and even what may be some possible consequences of his thinking and sayings.

Beside the more direct interpretation and exposition of the ideas of Gregory and of what is stated more explicitly in his writings there is thus an interpretation and discussion made of what might be possible implications in or of his thinking. There are even some attempts made to do what might be called a further interpretation out of or upon the ideas and formulations of Gregory. I have, in this way, wished to show some ideas which are possible to draw as consequences of the saying of Gregory or which we in an other way perhaps even should regard as unarticulated implications inherent in his thinking. When such an interpretation is made this is cleary stated in the study. The possibility of this, to a certain degree, owes to Gregory's way of expressing and formulating himself. Namely that he has got a special ability to express himself with rather short but expressive formulations which easily remain in the mind of the listener or the reader. In the main texts presented in the third chapter we have got a good example of this. Here Gregory expresses himself with a lot of short formulations, sometimes accumulating quite a number of them. The brevity of the formulations perhaps even together with the number of them in some of the passages, contributes to a certain suggestive character to the texts. This means that besides that which is actually stated, the passages open themselves for the associations and further thinking of the reader.

Such a "further" interpretation on the basis of Gregory's thinking is, for example, that which concerns the "first", original man. His situation here even before the fall is understood as the one of someone before a decision, who has not yet made up his mind. Further this may be interpreted as to concern man as such and his earthly life, quite apart from the fact whether he is fallen or not. And so the earthly life of man might be understood as the place for an inevitable decision that belongs to the personal existence as such.[18]

6. The literature on Gregory of Nazianzus

There is a rather large amount of literature on Gregory of Nazianzus and his writings studied from different points of view[19] though not so much among it is dealing directly with his theology.[20] The anthropology and spirituality are the objects of some studies[21] among which especially three should be mentioned here, namely H. Althaus, *Die Heilslehre des heiligen Gregor von Nazianz*, F. Portmann, *Die göttliche Paidagogia bei Gregor von Nazianz* and Th. Spidlík, *Grégoire de Nazianze, Introduction à l'étude de sa doctrine spirituelle*. In some respects this study overlaps these three works and sometimes the discussion will be held with the opinions of these authors. In especially the two later books by F. Portmann and T. Spidlík, beside the more direct discussion of the ideas of Gregory, we even find some different Hellenistic ideas dealth with which are found in the thinking of Gregory, for example, the Greek idea of "paideia" or the understanding of man as a "microcosm". The presence of the first idea in the thinking of Gregory, that of a divine "paideia" or pedagogy on man by God in salvation as well as in creation, is the special theme of the very good and valuable study by Portmann. In this respect he talks about a pedagogical anthropology[22] and further talks about an "Urerziehung", a primal, primordial pedagogy of God on man given already with the creation as such. "Mit dem Urstand des Menschen verband der heilige Gregor also auch eine Urerziehung",[23] a theme which is also worked with in the second part of this study.

7. The material of the study, editions and translations

The material of this study is limited to the orations of Gregory (Or 1–45),[24] his dogmatic poems (*PD.* 1–38)[25] and the so called theological letters on the christological issue (Ep. 101, 102 and 202).[26] Thus most of the poems by Gregory as well as the most of his letters are left aside.

Of the 45 orations the 35th one is regarded as non authentic.[27] In F. Lefherz, *Studien zu Gregor von Nazianz*, an account is given for some of the dogmatic poems for which the authenticity has been questioned (nr. 12, 28, 29, 32 and 37).[28] None of these poems have been used for this study.

The editions[29] used are the one of Migne (*PG* 35–37) together with the present text critical editions. Thus Or 1–3, 20–23, 27–31 and Ep. 101, 102 and 202 are published in modern text critical editions in the series, *Sources Chrétiennes*.

In regard to translations, almost all the orations are covered by the different collections of the orations by Gregory. The critical edition of the three theological letters in the series, *Sources Chrétiennes*, even offers a translation and finally extracts of the dogmatic poems are found in P. Gallay, *Grégoire de Nazianze, Poèmes et lettres*, p. 126–138.

Chapter 2
Man as a spiritual and bodily being

1. The doubleness[1] of man

For Gregory of Nazianzus man is a double being[2] made up by body and soul, spirit and flesh. When God made man, Gregory says in his second oration, he mingled "dust with spirit and compounded a living being, visible and invisible, temporal and immortal, earthly and heavenly. . ."[3]

This doubleness of man, a spiritual as well as a material and earthly being, is a characteristic feature in the anthropology of Gregory and we here find two important aspects from which he regards man and his existence.

As stated in the passage before, man is formed of dust and spirit. He is a bit of earth[4] to which the soul an inbreathing of God is joined.[5] Talking about this doubleness of man, Gregory, sometimes in antithetical language, is using some characteristic attributes or qualities by means of which he contrasts the two "components" or aspects of man. He is visible and invisible, earthly and heavenly, mortal and immortal, low and high.[6] We find Gregory underlining the doubleness of man by way of contrast.

Thanks to this doubleness man further might be said to belong to two different worlds or spheres, the material as well as the spiritual and heavenly. "I am small and great, lowly and high, mortal and immortal, earthly and heavenly. The one condition I share with this world below, the other with God, the one with the flesh, the other with the spirit."[7]

We often find Gregory contrasting these two spheres the heavenly and the earthly, of which the one is firm and stable and the other unstable and changing.[8] Sometimes this means a more direct contrasting of the earthly to God himself,[9] sometimes just a contrasting of the earthly and heavenly spheres.[10]

Here, in the understanding and thinking of Gregory on reality, we find featured a kind of basic dualism which conditions much of his thinking. The meaning here of this term, dualism, is a) an understanding of reality as consisting of two kinds of natures or spheres or qualities, matter and spirit, which includes b) an understanding of the spiritual reality as being of a higher value than the material one, though the latter is not necessarily to be regarded as evil, only lower than the spiritual one.

So Gregory might be said to reckon with two contrasted realities or spheres to which man as a double being belongs, the material as well as the spiritual.

2. The text on creation in Or. 38.9—11

For the further discussion we shall start with a longer passage from Or. 38. 9—11. This text is one of the few where Gregory gives a longer treatise on the creative act of God.[11] (The same text is found in Or. 45.5—8.)

Here we are told about the creation and giving of existence by God to the two worlds, the intelligible and the material ones, and to man as a kind of mingling of the two kinds of natures, the material and the spiritual. First the spiritual world is created, then the material one and at last man as a kind of bringing together of the two first kinds of qualities or natures. As the passage is one of the essential ones it will be rendered in its complete form.

Having talked about God in his eternal existence as the "existing one",[12] Gregory goes on.

Or. 38.9—11

(9) "Since this movement of selfcontemplation alone was not enough for the goodness but good must be poured out and go forth so that the objects of its kindness might be more (for this was fitting to the highest Goodness), he first conceived the angelic and heavenly powers. And this conception was a work fulfilled by the Word and perfected by the Spirit. And so the secondary splendours came into being, ministers of the primary Splendour, whether we are to understand them as intelligent (*νοερός*) spirits or as a kind of immaterial and incorporeal fire, or as some other nature which is as near as possible to this. I wish to say that they were incapable of movement towards evil and only able of the movement of good as being near God and as the first illumined by Him. For these here [on earth] have only the secondary illumination. But I am pursuaded to think and talk of them not as incapable but difficult to move [towards evil] because of him, who was Lucifer because of his splendour, but became and was called darkness because of his pride, and the rebellious powers under him, authors of evil by their escape from good and our inciters.

(10) So and for these reasons the intelligible (*νοητός*) world came into being as far as I can investigate into these matters and estimate great things with a small reason. Then when the first [creation] was good to him, he conceived a second world, material and visible. And this is the system and compound of sky and earth and that between them, praiseworthy for the fair form of every part but yet more worthy to be praised for the harmony and unison of all, one part well fitting in with the whole to the completion of one world. This was to show that he was able to make to exist not only a nature akin (*οἰκεῖος*) to himself but even one altogether strange (*ξένος*).

18

For akin to deity are those natures which are intellectual and only to be comprehended by mind. But entirely strange is all that [is known] by perception by the senses, and of these all those are yet furthest off which are wholly without soul and incapable of motion. ...

(11) Mind then and sense, in this way separated from each other, remained within their own bounderies and bore in themselves the magnificence of the Creator Word, silent praisers of his mighty work and thrilling heralds. Not yet was there any mixture of both nor any mingling of these opposites, token of a greater wisdom and generosity concerning the natures. Nor was the whole richness of goodness known. Now the Creator Word wanting to show this and [to produce] one living being (ζῶον ἕν) of both, I mean the invisible and visible nature, creates man. And taking the body from the already existing matter, and placing in it a breath from himself (which the Word knew to be an intelligent soul [νοερὰ ψυχή] and an image of God), as a kind of second world. Great in little he placed him on the earth, another angel, a mingled worshipper, fully initiated (ἐπόπτης) into the visible creation but only partially (μύστης) into the intellectual. A king of that on earth, ruled from above, earthly and heavenly, temporal and immortal, visible and intellectual (νοούμενος), midway between greatness and lowliness, at the same time spirit and flesh (ὁ αὐτός, πνεῦμα καὶ σάρξ), spirit because of the grace, flesh because of the pride. The one that he might continue to live and to give honour to his benefactor. The other that he might suffer and suffering be reminded and corrected if he became proud of his greatness. A living being ruled here and moved elsewhere and to complete the mystery, deified by his inclination to God. For to this I think, tends the light of truth [which we posses] here in measure, to see and experience the splendour of God, which is worthy of him who bound us together and will dissolve and bind us together again loftier."

In this passage we are first told how God is creating a spiritual, non-material world. This is made up of heavenly and angelic powers and is called an intelligible world. These powers is a kind of "secondary" splendour illumined by God and being near to him.

Thereafter the material, visible world is created as a system and compound of that which is on earth and in the sky and in between. This second world is talked about in a positive way, which should not be forgotten even though it is so emphatically contrasted to the first, spiritual one. It is worthy of praise and Gregory speaks about its harmony and fair order. Doing this, God shows that he is not only able to create something akin (οἰκεῖος) to himself and we might even say familiar, but also something strange or different (ξένος). In this way Gregory points out the nearness of the spiritual world to God in comparison with an inferred distance of the material one, the things "wholly without soul and incapable of motion" are spoken of as furthest off from God.

These two kinds of natures still existed separately from each other. Gregory further says that they "bore in themselves the magnificence of the Creator Word, silent praisers of his mighty work and thrilling heralds". This is even said about the material creation, which Gregory just has talked about as strange to God.

Gregory continues by talking about the creation of man as a bringing together and blending of these two kinds of natures or qualities. Through this God further shows his greatness and goodness in the bringing together of these two opposite natures or qualities.

It should first be observed that the soul of man according to the telling of Gregory not is taken from the already existing spiritual world but is understood as completely, newly created by God, "a breath from himself". When Gregory talks about a bringing together in man of "mind" and "sense" this should not be literally understood as a bringing together of the two worlds, the material and that of the angels, that already existed but separate. It is rather a uniting of the two kinds of natures that already existed. We might talk about a uniting "in principle" of the two kinds of natures in man.

Man is here described as a compound being made up by two different and opposite components and through an enumeration of the qualities of these two components this is emphasized. He is "earthly and heavenly, temporal and immortal, visible and intellectual. . .". So man is understood as being made up of two different and opposite elements.

3. The spiritual, intelligible world

The spiritual world is sometimes by Gregory just called "tà nooúmena",[13] that which by "noús" or mind is seen and comprehended. It is the intelligible, "noetic" world or sphere to which man, as an intellectual being, belongs. This world is often spoken of by Gregory in categories of light. It is a sphere of light, where God is the first light, from which light is going forth, surrounded by a heavenly world of angels, a kind of second light illumined by God.[14]

A third light is man, Gregory says in the text which the following passage is taken from. "God is the highest light. . . in a small degree pouring himself out upon what is external. That light I mean which is contemplated in the Father and the Son and the Holy Spirit . . . A second light is the angel, a kind of outflow of or participation in the first light having its illumination through its inclination and service thereto."[15]

In spite of the emanative language it is quite clear that Gregory was thinking of this "second light" as a created world.[16] In Or. 38.9 we meet the description of this creation.

20

This world of angels is near God, though Gregory in some texts even knows about a kind of distance between God and the angels,[17] and I even think Gregory understood them as surrounding God.[18] As to their nature, the angels are talked about as intelligible spirits or a kind of immaterial fire. They are almost immovable in direction towards evil and Gregory would have preferred to think of them as immovable and incapable of evil if it was not for Lucifer or Satan who fell because of his pride.[19] For probably the same reason Gregory, in spite of all, seems to have had to ascribe them some kind of materiality.[20]

As to function, the angels are receivers of the beneficence of God, as it belongs to the nature of God to have objects for his goodness. They are the servants of the will of God and "hymners of the divine Majesty, eternally contemplating the eternal glory". In the same text, Or. 28.31, they are even said to be, thanks to their nearness to the first light, God, a kind of second light able to illumine others with that which is coming from the first light. They are thus talked about as some kind of intermediaries of the light of God, and, in the poem on the spirits, Gregory even talks about a protection of the world by the angels.[21]

When Gregory is talking about this spiritual world it is not always, quite clear if he is thinking of God or the spiritual creation. Perhaps sometimes he is just thinking of the whole intelligible context and the sphere of light toward which man, thanks to his own share of light,[22] is inclined.

4. Body and soul, spirit and flesh

Even man is thus called "light".[23] But, during his earthly life he has only partly received a share of it.[24] He is not as the angels "near" the first light but at a distance from God.[25] In spite of the fact that he is an earthly being, he longs for the fuller light of the heavenly life. As previously stated, it is just these two aspects of man as both an earthly and a heavenly being, that are mirrored in Gregory's main view on man as "double" and compounded from two elements.

For these two components of man Gregory is using varying terms. Man is body ($\sigma\tilde{\omega}\mu\alpha$) and soul ($\psi\upsilon\chi\dot{\eta}$),[26] he is flesh ($\sigma\acute{\alpha}\rho\xi$) and spirit ($\pi\nu\varepsilon\tilde{\upsilon}\mu\alpha$).[27] He is made up by earth united to a breath of God.[28] (Genesis 2:7) These terms are not used completely synonymously. Without being quite consistent, for the concrete, actual body and soul of man, Gregory is using the first couple of terms while "flesh" and "spirit" more are denoting the two aspects or characteristics that are man's.[29] Sometimes though, soul and spirit are quite synonymously used, whereas in some texts the spirit is opposed to the "dust" in a way which concerns the attitude on life.[30]

Generally, Gregory talks about man as a double being but he uses a trichotomy or even a four-partite division of man when talking about "soul and mind" or "soul, mind and reason".[31]

21

5. The soul of man

5.a. A divine origin

For Gregory the soul of man is something divine and heavenly.[32] It is, he says in Or. 2.17 "from God and divine and partakes of the nobility above, and hastens to it even if it is bound together with the inferior [nature]". Sometimes Gregory with the language of Genesis 2:7 talks about the soul as a breath of God.[33] In the poem on the soul we find him yet more strongly expressing the divinity of man when talking about the spirit which "is a piece broken off the invisible deity"[34] and in Or. 14.7 he talks in a similar way about we who are "a part of God".[35]

These formulations seem to express an emanative understanding. Gregory though, clearly thinks of man as created.[36] This will further be discussed in chapter 4. But what I want to point out here is what might be called a divine origin of man. The soul belongs to the divine sphere already by its origin.

5.b. The turning upwards of the soul

The divinity of the soul and its divine origin points to its destiny. Man has "an inclination to God".[37]

Before going on, I think it should be stated that this divine destiny of man concerns man as a being of both body and soul. Even if Gregory, with the Platonizing tradition, talks about the soul of man that should be released from the burdering and impeding flesh in order to seek what is "above", this is not the only aspect of flesh and matter in his thinking. The heavenly goal which the soul is longing for is even the goal of the flesh.[38] This will be discussed in more detail further on, but should be mentioned already here.

The turning "upwards" of the soul away from the flesh though is a strong motif in the writings of Gregory[39] and in Platonic language he talks about the soul directing itself towards God on the wings of mind or reason.[40] In Or. 21 he talks about God as the object for the desire of man, "So God, who creates for those who think (νοεῖν) and for that which is thought of [the ability of] thinking and being thought of, is Himself the highest of that which is thought of, in Whom every desire finds its bourne, and beyond Whom it in no way can go.

For not even the most philosophical mind, or the most penetrating, or the most curious has or shall ever have something higher [as object]. For this is the outmost of things desirable and there is for those who arrive [at it] a rest from all speculation.

Whoever who through reason and contemplation keeping apart from matter and this fleshly cloud or veil (whichever it should be called) has been allowed to be with God and be mixed with the purest light as far as the human nature can attain, is blessed both for his ascent hence from, and for his deification there, which is granted through true philosophy and through rising above the material duality through the unity which is perceived in the Trinity".[41] In this passage, which is a very typical one, God is presented as the goal that is above everything else, and the one is praised who has turned himself away from matter and flesh. In another typical text Gregory talks about providing "the soul with wings, to carry it off from the world and give it to God and take care of that which is according to the image. . .".[42]

Reading these and similar texts I think it should be observed that the point of the texts not only or even mainly is the idea that the soul of man should be released from the body and the flesh which is so much "lower" than the spirit. The emphasis is just as much on that which is the goal of the soul and the object of its desire and longing, namely God. There is a strong love for God and the divine in the writings of Gregory. This has an attraction.

5.c. The intellectual, spiritual and rational character of man

For Gregory, man is an intellectual, spiritual and rational being ($\nu o\varepsilon\rho\acute{o}\varsigma$, $\lambda o\gamma\iota\kappa\acute{o}\varsigma$).[43] These characteristics, being an intellectual and spiritual being, to a certain extent may be regarded main aspects of man in the thinking of Gregory or even as the main ones, to a certain degree being related to all the other aspects discussed in this paragraph about the soul of man.

What now is the meaning of this character? If we talk about man as an intellectual being, the emphasis is not on the ability of man to a knowledge about the created world, or to reflect on and think about the creation, but on a knowledge about God and on knowing and experiencing of Him. Through his intellectual and spiritual character man belongs to the spiritual, "noetic" world or sphere. He might be said to have an affinity for it. So we may say that in this character of man Gregory is seeing not only the base for man's knowledge about God but even for his communication with God, and his possibility to come "near" to God and into contact with him. In this affinity is the possibility for like to meet like, and for "theoria", contemplation and "seeing" of God.[44]

As already mentioned Gregory alongside with the basic dichotomy of man as made up by soul and body uses the trichotomy of body, soul and mind and even a four-partite division of body, soul, mind and reason.[45] (The terminology is not quite consistent.)

Of the different "parts" of the soul, the mind ($\nu o\tilde{\upsilon}\varsigma$) of man may be regarded as a wider notion than the reason or the intellect ($\lambda\acute{o}\gamma o\varsigma$, even $\delta\iota\acute{a}\nu o\iota a$).[46] The mind is sometimes called the "leading" or "governing" ($\dot{\eta}\gamma\varepsilon\mu\acute{\omega}\nu$) within man[47] and is generally thought about as a "part" or function of the soul but is sometimes used more or less synonomously with the soul. "Diánoia" or "lógos" might be understood as the rational part or instrument of the soul (with the wings of the intellect man or the soul is rising towards God),[48] though the use of all these terms is not totally fixed or coherent.

As already stated the rationality of man is related to his relation to God and to the contemplation and experience of the divine,[49] for which he has a previous disposition in his "noetic" character. It is even worth noticing that this contemplation of God in many texts is associated with an important degree of nearness to God and community with him. Thus the "knowing" of God in many passages is talked about in terms meaning, "be with", "converse with" or even "mix with".[50] Even the "personal" character of these terms should be noticed.

Summarizing the intellectual character of man, it might be said to refer to his relation to God and his belonging to the "noetic" sphere. As concerning a knowledge of God, it is a knowledge that is associated with an experience of the object and a communication. We have seen that Gregory, talking about man's contemplation of God, even uses terms with the meaning of community and nearness. It is even a knowing which is joined with a longing for God and a desire for him. "... where there is purifying, there is illumination; And illumination is the fulfilment of the desire for those who long for the greatest things or the greatest or that which is beyond greatness."[51]

5.d. The image of God

Gregory shares the idea of the early church of man as the image of God (Genesis 1: 26). "I am myself an image ($\varepsilon i\kappa\omega\nu$) of God, of the glory above, even if I am placed here below."[52] What now is the meaning of this likeness to God and of the idea that man shall be "like God" ($\vartheta\varepsilon o\varepsilon\iota\delta\eta\varsigma$)[53]?

First it should be mentioned that this character of man refers to the soul of man and not to his body. In creating man God unites the soul of man, the image, to a body formed by earth. "The one who mixed knows how he first breathed and bound the image to [a bit of] earth".[54] Sometimes the image refers to the rational part of the soul[55] but generally it just refers to the soul as such.

The term which Gregory is using for the image is the word "eikón". We thus in the writings of Gregory do not find the well known distinction between image ($\varepsilon i\kappa\omega\nu$) and likeness ($\delta\mu o\iota\omega\sigma\iota\varsigma$)[56] referring to a distinction between a likeness (image) already given in the creation and a likeness ($\delta\mu o\iota\omega\sigma\iota\varsigma$) attained through the growth of man and his own effort.

Now I think though that we are right to postulate that Gregory was thinking in line with this tradition without using the terminology just referred to. What points in this direction are some different facts and circumstances.

a) First the fact that Gregory counted on an original immaturity of the primal man as will be discussed in the next chapter.

b) It is even possible to notice the use of another term, namely "$\vartheta\varepsilon o\varepsilon\iota\delta\eta\varsigma$", "like God", which Gregory is using (though not consistently) for what man shall obtain through his purification and Christian life, and which in some texts is related to his final state.[57]

c) In a dynamic way in some texts, Gregory further talks about man's "preservation of the image" and his "ἐξομοίωσις", that is his assimilation to God or "becoming like God".[58] Now this "assimilation" might only be understood as a regaining of an original likeness to God lost in the fall of man. What makes this unlikely is though what is said above about man's original and primal immaturity and also the fact that Gregory understood man as a free being, who himself should inherit and gain "the good" and even life with God which will be discussed further on. These circumstances, I think, now give us the right to read Gregory against the background of the tradition referred to above and count him within it.

Generally, Gregory talks about man as the image or the image of God, but sometimes he makes another distinction. He then talks about man who is "κατ' εἰκόνα",[59] "according to" or "after the image". The image here refers to Christ as the image of God[60] and man is the one who is "according" to him. "Let us give back to the image that which is according to the image".[61] The one who man is "like", God, is in this context called "τὸ ἀρχέτυπον", archetype or model.[62]

What now is the meaning of this characteristic of man and what is the content of the term image? Gregory never directly answers this or presents us with any definitions. Nevertheless I think we are right to say that the "image" of God refers to what has already been said in this chapter about the soul of man. It refers to his divinity and to his intellectual and spiritual character, and is sometimes mentioned together with the high dignity of man (ἀξίωμα).[63]

At last it should be noticed that in speaking about the image of God and about man becoming like God Gregory relates this more to the relationship to God and to the coming life than to the life on earth and the material life.[64] The likeness of God is thus more related to what will be discussed in next paragraph about the goal of man and his divinisation than to his position and rank as the image of God on earth. Perhaps we would expect reflections and thinking on the mission and task of man as king on earth being the image of God, but this is not the main interest of Gregory.

So when Gregory talks about the image of God, he is often doing it with reference to the salvation and deification of man and to what Christ and the Spirit are doing for man. "This is for us the purpose of the great mystery, this [is the purpose] for us of God who for us was incarnated and became poor, that he might raise our flesh, and recover the image, and form man anew, that we all might become one in Christ who became in all of us all that he himself is, that we might no longer be male and female, barbarian and Scythian, slave and free, which are the marks of the flesh, but might only bear in ourselves the divine stamp (χαρακτήρ) of which and to which we have become, and have so far received our form and model from him that we are known by it alone."[65]

5.e. The final goal of man and his god-becoming

We shall so in this last paragraph about the soul of man, stop at the final goal and state of man as Gregory understands it. In Or. 38.11 he talks about man who will be deified "by his inclination to God. For to this I think tends the light of truth [which we posses] here in measure, to see and experience the splendour of God".

In another oration, Or. 16.9, Gregory in a similar manner talks about the resurrection and the heavenly life of man when "some will be received by the unutterable light and the contemplation of the holy and royal Trinity, enlightening more clear and pure and wholly mingling Itself with the whole mind, in which solely and beyond else I hold the kingdom of heaven to be."

In these and other texts we find some different aspects of the final goal of man as Gregory talks about it. To start with we may observe the idea of knowing God and an experience of him which in many texts are talked about in categories of light.[66] This knowing and seeing of God has already been discussed from the aspect of man as an intellectual and spiritual being.

Gregory further speaks of a divinisation ($\vartheta \acute{\varepsilon} \omega \sigma \iota \varsigma$)[67] of man, when man will "become god" or "be made god" and God himself be as God amongst gods.[68] If we now ask what this "théosis"[69] of man is and what it means that man will "be god" we must take notice that this is a case where Gregory talks more about "how" man is being deified and how it is made possible than about the content of it. (It is evident though that Gregory not was thinking literally of "man-becoming-god". In Or. 42.17 he thus states that man not will become god properly speaking.)

Reading the texts we find two things that are related to the "god-becoming" of man. First, it is made possible by the Son and the Spirit, and further it is associated with the incarnation and "man-becoming" of Christ (and here "man-becoming" very emphatically means a taking on by God of all that is human, both body and soul, and mind[70]).

The divinisation is thus associated with the Son and the Spirit and their work. In Or. 2.22 Gregory talks about the making of Christ ". . . to dwell in the hearts through the Spirit, and summarizing, to make to god. . ."[71]

In several texts where Gregory is defending the divinity of the Spirit he states further that the Spirit would not be able to make a human being God if he himself was not God. "If He is in the same rank with me, how does He make me god? Or how does He join me to the deity?"[72]

The "god-making" of man is further associated with the incarnation. In the Third Theological Oration, we find the classical formula about God becoming man "in order that I may become god so far as he has become man".[73] Also on another occasion, he talks about man becoming god through the incarnation.[74]

It should so be noted that Gregory does not talk so much directly about theosis as a participation in the divine nature or a unification with God.[75]

At last it should be added that Gregory in some texts even talks about a change and a renovation of the material world in the coming life. In Or. 7.21 he thus talks about "the change of the form of heaven, the reformation of the earth, the liberation of the elements, the renewal of the whole universe."[90]

6.c. The body of man

Gregory talks about the body of man both as friend and enemy. Generally however, he regards the body as something burdening and toilsome. In Or. 14, for which the theme is the love to the poor and distressed, in a longer passage and in an antithetic manner, Gregory expresses his mixed attitudes and feelings towards the body. ". . . this troublesome and low and faithless body, with which I don't know how I have been yoked together, and not how I both am an image of God and blended with the mud. [The body] that makes war when it is in good condition and grieves when war is made upon it, that I love as a fellow servant and turn away from as an enemy, that I even flee from as a fetter and honour as a joint heir. I strive to weaken it and don't know whom I may use as a cooperator for the best, knowing for what I have been made and that I ought to ascend to God through my actions.

I use [it] sparingly as cooperator and don't know how I may escape its insurrection, or how I may not fall from God weighed down by its fetters which draw [me] down or keep [me] back to the ground. It is a gracious enemy and a treacherous friend. O, such union (συζυγία) and such separation (ἀλλοτρίωσις, alt. estrangement). What I fear I treat with respect and of that which I love I am afraid. Before I make war I reconcile myself, and before I make peace I set myself at variance with it."[91]

The body causes troubles not only because of diseases and what else it might cause to man. But, there is even in man something that might be called an inverted order which means that the soul of man no longer is ruling the lower body. Gregory therefore urges his readers to follow the spirit and not the flesh.

Man in his desire to know or "see" God is further hindered by what is called the "veil" of the body and its "grossness".

6.d. An inverted order

Follow the spirit and not the flesh Gregory often exhorts.[92] Behind this attitude we find not only the understanding of the spiritual as being of so much higher value than the material, but even that idea of what might be called an inverted order. In man, the soul should rule the body.[93] When the soul, or the mind of man which sometimes is understood as the ruling instrument within man,[94] gives up its ruling function the door is open for a kind of disorder. We could even interpret Gregory as meaning that the interest of man has been turned in the wrong direction, away from its spiritual and heavenly goal, towards that which belongs to this world and to the flesh.

Closely related to this is even the understanding of the body as the seat of passions.[95] Gregory I think though counts even on spiritual passions. The whole of man is in need of a cleansing. So he can, in Or. 37.22, say "Cut off the bodily (σωματικός) passions, cut also off the spiritual (ψυχικός)."

6.e. Hinderance for the knowing and "seeing" of God

A dominant aspect in Gregory's understanding of the body is what might be labelled the body as a hindrance in the knowing or "seeing" of God. The body or flesh of man for Gregory has got a kind of "grossness" or "coarseness" (παχύτης, thickness, grossness).[96] In some texts this "grossness" is talked about as something that keeps man back from the knowing of God. In Or. 28. 12 this grossness is talked about as a kind of darkness which is an obstacle for the seeing of God.[97] The flesh sometimes even is talked about as a cloud or veil between man and God.[98] The body of man is thus an impediment for him, "... between us and God this bodily darkness is placed".[99] In a similar way Gregory sometimes even is talking about the "fetters" of the body which keep down the soul, which on the wings of reason wants to rise towards God.[100]

This attitude of Gregory to the body as "veil" and "fetters" should be understood in relation to his main idea about man as a being made for a spiritual life and for a knowing and an experiencing of God. This knowing is a question of the contemplation of a wholly spiritual object which only might be perceived by the spirit or mind of man,[101] and in this respect man now is a captive in his dense body and kept back from the object for which he has a natural desire. This is the background before which I think many of the negative sayings of Gregory about the body should be understood. For the soul, which is strongly longing for God, the body is a painful obstacle which—through its very existence hinders contemplation, rendering it difficult.[102]

It might be discussed whether Gregory meant that a full knowledge of God ever will be possible for man. In this life however, he regarded it as impossible. Man is always bound to his body and the senses and the knowledge given by them.[103]

Dealing with the "grossness" of the flesh a certain problem at last imposes itself, namely whether Gregory regarded this "grossness" as originally given to man or something resulting from the fall of the primal man, Adam. This is a question which we generally don't find explicitly answered.

In Or. 38.12, though Gregory talks about the original man who "was naked in his simplicity and his inartificial life and without any covering or defence", and comments on the biblical story. He states further that Adam after the fall "put on the coats of skins, that is perhaps an even denser flesh (τὴν παχυτέραν σάρκα) both mortal and contradictory". Or, with an alternative translation

30

where the comparative "*παχυτέραν*" is understood as having an absolute meaning rather than a relative, Adam might be understood to have put on "the coats of skins, the very (alt too or rather) dense flesh".

From our point of view the text now has got a certain ambiguity talking about an original nakedness of man (which might be understand as a more moral one, rather than specifically dealing with his body) and his flesh becoming "denser" after the fall, or if we choose the alternative translation, man getting a "very dense" flesh after the fall. So we may understand Gregory either thinking about an original grossness of the flesh getting yet denser after the fall of man, or aiming at an original state without any grossness at all.[104]

In another text, Or. 28.12, which will be discussed later in more detail,[105] Gregory, as I understand him though, clearly seems to regard the "grossness" of the flesh as original and given to man from the beginning.

For Gregory the primordial man, Adam was, as will even be discussed in the next chapter, an immature being who did not fully see God and kept away from the full contemplation of him.[106] This understanding of Gregory of the original immaturity of man now makes it likely that he regarded the "grossness" of the flesh as originally something that is a given with man and not a consequence of the fall.

6.f. The resurrection and the change of the bodily character

Even if the turning "upwards" of the soul away from flesh and matter is a dominant motif in the writings of Gregory there is never a question of a salvation from the body. The heavenly goal is even the goal of the body of man. The Word of God "partakes of my flesh that he may both save the image and make the flesh immortal".[107] The body is talked about as the fellowheir of the soul,[108] and in Or. 2.17, Gregory is saying that the soul shall draw the body to itself "and place the inferior one above, gradually freeing it from its grossness in order that the soul may be to the body what God is to the soul, through itself leading its assistant matter and intimating it to God, as fellow servant."

In this passage as in some others we even find something expressed which might be called a kind of mission of the soul vis-à-vis the body. So Gregory states in Or. 16.15: ". . . may the image cleanse the mud, and place its yoke-fellow, the flesh, above, raising it on the wings of reason."[109]

Gregory further seems to reckon with a change of the corporeality in the heavenly existence of man when the body shall be free from its grossness and the deadly character[110] (texts on this theme are very few though). On the occasion of the death of his brother, Caesarius,[111] Gregory speaks about the body of man and the future state and relation of the soul to the body. Freed from the body through death, the soul enters the heavenly life and good . . . But this is even the lot of the body, and so the soul ". . . just as it had a share in its hardships (e.g. the body's) through the union (*συμφυΐα*), so it also gives a share

31

[to the body] of its own pleasures, absorbing it entirely into itself, and becoming with it one, both spirit and mind and god,[112] the mortal and mutable being swallowed up by the life."[113]

Gregory so goes on to talk about the re-formation ($\mu\varepsilon\tau\alpha\pi o\acute{\iota}\eta\sigma\iota\varsigma$) of the earth and the renewal ($\dot{\alpha}\nu\alpha\kappa\alpha\acute{\iota}\nu\iota\sigma\iota\varsigma$) of the whole universe when Caesarius will be "no longer in exile, ... brilliant, glorious, lofty".[114]

At last he turns himself to the mystery of Christ and talks about the deification of man and about a change of the bodily character. Christ has become man that he might "raise our flesh and recover the image and form man anew" and that we might no longer bear the marks of the flesh, e.g. sex or nationality, "but might only bear in ourselves the divine stamp..."[115]

What we here find is talk of a change in the body's character, and of a body no longer mortal and no longer with particular characteristics, like sex or nationality. The texts even might be understood as aiming at a divine character given to the body, and perhaps we may say that Gregory in this oration is talking about a kind of divinisation of the body.

The very strong formulations on the relationship of the soul to the body after death in this text should be noted. The soul will be with the flesh "one, both spirit and mind and god"[116]. This union is talked about as an absorbing of the body and the fleshly characteristics. The soul "is absorbing it entirely into itself"[117] and Gregory further speaks about "the mortal and the mutable being swallowed up by life".[118] However, Gregory does not expect any final disappearing or consuming of the body though. That is clear from the other passages referred to in this paragraph.

Summarizing from these texts (even though they are rather few), we may say that Gregory seems to think of a changed corporeality of man in his heavenly existence. In Or. 7 he describes what might be understood as a highly spiritual or spiritualized body. We recall that a characteristic mark of the earthly body of man is its "grossness" ($\pi\alpha\chi\acute{\upsilon}\tau\eta\varsigma$), which hinders man in his knowing of God. In the final state man will be freed in this respect,[119] and we may consequently understand him as able to contemplate God being without the denseness or opaqueness of the flesh.

6.g. The relation of the material world to God

We shall conclude this section with the understanding of Gregory as to the relationship of the material world and creation to God and the doubleness of this relationship consisting of both nearness and testimony as well as distance and difference.

That which concerns his relationship to the creation which he has brought into existence, is spoken about as God's maintainance of the world. He holds it together and takes care of it. So in Or.28.6, he is talked about as "the efficient and maintaining cause" of all. In another oration, the Word of God (the Son) is said to exist in that which exists and is called "power as the preserver of all created things and as providing them with the power of keeping together".[120] Gregory further counts upon a presence of God in all the creation. God "is in all and outside all",[121] he "pervades and fills all things".[122]

The visible creation further bears witness to God. In Or. 38.11 Gregory says that the newly created material creation, as well as the spiritual, "bore in themselves the magnificence of the Creator Word, silent praisers of his mighty work and thrilling heralds."[123]

In the same oration though we find the visible creation even talked about as wholly strange (ξένος, strange, different, separate) to God, in difference to the spiritual natures which were familiar to him or akin to him, (οἰκεῖος, belonging to, akin).[124] We have even seen how emphatically the material world is often contrasted by Gregory to the spiritual one.

In the passage just referred to, Or. 38.10, Gregory discusses further the material natures known by the senses, and says that "of these all those are yet furthest off which are wholly without soul and incapable of motion." What we here find is a reference to a kind of distance to God with regard to the material creation. It is evident from a number of texts that Gregory, for the most part, was thinking of the material creation, including man, as being at a kind of distance from God as in contrast to the nearness of the spiritual heavenly creation and being further away from God than this latter.[125]

In the Christology of Gregory we find an example of what might be called an ontological difference between divine and material. So the soul or mind of Christ is understood as having a kind of middle position in him between his flesh and his divine nature and a mediating function.[126]

It should perhaps also be mentioned that Gregory on the other hand though, on some occasions, talks about the body of Christ as a means through which God is made known to man. He is "God visible".[127]

Thus, Gregory thinks both of nearness and distance that concerns the relationship of the world to God. These two aspects are found side by side and there is no attempt by Gregory to do any systematizing here. There is one text here though that should be mentioned where we find Gregory making a certain distinction of interests. The passage is found in Or. 28.3, an oration for which a central theme is the knowing of God and the possibilities and limits of a knowledge of him. Here Gregory distinguishes between that of God which is known only to God's self (his nature, if this is the proper reading and understanding of the text), and that which reaches to us. The latter is the majesty (μεγαλειότης), which is "among the creatures and that which is produced and governed by him." And this is the "back parts of God", his "tokens" like "the reflections of the sun in water". Gregory finally summarizes by saying that the heavenly things are farther away from God and the perfect comprehension than they are lifted above us. Thus a kind of distinction between the incomprehensible God and that of him which reaches to us, his majesty and tokens, expressed in terms of distance and presence or nearness.

The relation of the material world to God is marked by difference and distance. At last it should be noticed that, as we have discussed before,[128] Gregory in some respects counts with a kind of change and diminishing of this difference and distance. The changing and instable world will once be changed into a state of stability[129] and the body of man will be released from its grossness and brought to God together with the soul of man becoming with it "one, both spirit and mind and god".[130]

In one of the orations, Or. 30, we even find an idea not expressed elsewhere. Here Gregory with biblical language talks about the time of restitution when all will be subjected to Christ, the Son, and the Son will subject all to the Father, and when further "God shall be all in all".[131] Here we systematically may speak about a final abolition of the distance between the material world, the creation, and God. If we now compare this to the sayings of Gregory in Or. 28.3 discussed above, we should perhaps understand him in that passage to talk about an outermost distance that never will be abolished.

6.h. The double attitude towards the material world and creation

As previously noted, Gregory's outlook on the material creation and on the earthly and bodily life of man is sometimes, on one hand, a quite positive attitude, and sometimes, on the other hand, a negative one.[132] We may talk about a doubleness of his attitude. In this passage a discussion will be made of this double outlook on material reality and an attempt will be made to do an analysis of this doubleness of attitude. Is this double attitude a natural consequence of the thinking of Gregory in other respects and consistent with his theology as a whole? Or should we rather talk about a tension in his thinking between, on the one hand, the positive attitude and, on the other hand, the negative one?

In Gregory's understanding of the existing reality or realities, as noticed earlier,[133] we find a basic dualistic attitude. This dualism means a) an understanding of reality as consisting of two kinds of natures or spheres or qualities, matter and spirit, and b) further includes an understanding of the spiritual reality as being of a higher value than the material one.

Further we in the analysis of the theology of Gregory find something that we may describe and define as an ontological hierarchy, of course related to his dualistic outlook. This hierarchic understanding, which will be further discussed in chapter 4, means an understanding of the existing reality as consisting of two or three natures or spheres. Whether we should speak about two or three natures depends on the way we choose for a structuring of the ontology of Gregory. Either we may talk about three natures: 1) The divine, 2) the created, spiritual nature (the angels as well as the soul or spirit of man), 3) and at last the material reality to which the visible universe and the body of man belong, or we may talk about two kinds of natures or realities: 1) The spiritual one, consisting both of the uncreated divine nature, that is God Himself, and the created spiritual natures, 2) The material and visible world or nature.

This hierarchy even includes a scale of value and rank. The divine and spiritual reality is valued as higher than the material one. We have already in the beginning of this chapter met the antithetical way in which Gregory speaks about the spiritual and material realities and contrasts them.[134]

The ontological hierarchy of Gregory thus implies an attitude towards the different realities of the hierarchy. When we speak like this, about an ontology and an attitude which implies a valuation I think that we in the analysis of a theologian or a philosopher should be prepared to distinguish between a conscious attitude and an unconscious one which has not been reflected upon. Thus, we will make a distinction between, a) a conscious attitude which corresponds to an ontology and its conscious valuation and attitude, and b) an unconscious attitude not reflected upon, which not necessarily corresponds to the conscious and outspoken ontology and its valuation.

Gregory has a double attitude towards the material, visible nature of the world and existence. He can thus on one hand speak in a positive way about the visible, material world and creation. It is an admirable creation, worthy of praise, and it is ordered well and harmoniously. It is made for the enjoyment of man, and it is witness to God, its Creator. On the other hand, we find texts with a negative or even very negative attitude towards this visible and material world, and towards the bodily and earthly life of man. This world here below is a visible, unstable and changing world in contrast to the reality above, that which is firm and stable and permanent.

About this now following remarks can be made.

1) The two kinds of attitudes, the positive one and the negative one, to a certain degree are found in different kinds of passages and contexts. The positive attitude is found in texts which speak rather ontologically about the creation as the world created by God.[135] The other attitude, the negative one, is rather found in passages which speak spiritually and in an existential manner about the situation of man.[136]

2) Further the negative aspects in some passages by Gregory are explained as consequences of the fall of sin of the primal man. Through the original fall into sin there is a change for the worse.[137]

3) This (point 2) can only be regarded though as a partial answer. There is no doubt that Gregory also regarded this life as something originally troublesome and hard,[138] and that the material creation as such is contrasted to the spiritual one.

The negative attitude may then be seen as corresponding to his basic dualistic view and to his ontology with its hierarchy and rank of value. We can ascribe to Gregory such reasoning as follows. The material creation certainly is a good world and the good creation made by God, but in comparison to the spiritual world and that which is spiritual, the material reality must be looked upon as so much lower and as a lower form of reality. That which is material is a creation by God but foreign (ξένος) to him, in contrast to the spiritual creation that is akin to God or belongs to him (οἰκεῖος). With this we have a scale of value and man is missing his destiny if he keeps to that which is visible and unstable instead of that which is stable, invisible and spiritually conceived.

If we keep to what has been said so far the double attitude of Gregory might be said to be consistent with his theology and the discussion could be brought to an end here. I would though like to bring the discussion somewhat further, as I am not quite sure that the whole of the negative attitude of Gregory is completely "covered" and explained with what has been said so far. Thus, I will bring the discussion somewhat further even if this further discussion, by necessity, has a higher degree of uncertainty and a more hypothetic character.

The question can be formulated as following. Are the negative attitudes which Gregory often expresses in correspondence with his theology and ontology, as discussed under point 1—3 above, or does this negative attitude in reality go beyond his ontology and its conscious valuation?

This negative attitude Gregory shares with the Platonic or Platonizing tradition and at this point I want to bring his relationship to this tradition into the discussion.

First it should be stated that even within this tradition we find a doubleness what concerns the attitude to the visible and material reality. Further the attitude or attitudes are parts of a certain ontology and correspond to a certain understanding of the world. The visible world and universe in general is regarded as a well ordered world and cosmos. But, on the other hand, in this ordered and formed material world we find "hyle", or matter itself, the irrational, formless basic material of which everything is made. And this "hyle" is regarded in a more or less negative way in the Platonic tradition.[139] We may talk about a dark understanding of "hyle" and of matter as such.

In the Platonizing tradition we thus find a negative attitude towards the visible and material reality. This negative attitude corresponds to an ontology which implies a dark and negative attitude to "hyle" or to the basic material reality or substratum as such.

Gregory in his conscious ontology and theology must be understood to think of the visible, material reality as the good creation made by God.

At the same time, according to my understanding, Gregory shared his negative attitude towards the material reality with a tradition which in its basic ontology had a different understanding of matter itself and a "dark" understanding of hyle as discussed above.

What I wish to point out is that Gregory shares his attitude to the visible reality with a tradition which has a dark and negative attitude to hyle as such. An attitude which Gregory hardly may be understood to share consciously as

36

it concerns hyle or matter as such.[140]

This may now explain his sometimes highly negative sayings and attitudes, which at least according to my understanding, are in a certain tension to his more positive outlook on the material reality as God's wonderful creation.

Perhaps, as a concluding remark we should say that the Platonic or Hellenistic form of Christianity, which Gregory represents, by necessity implied a tension in regard to the outlook on earthly reality. Finally, at least this reader of Gregory, has to confess her difficulties with some of his more negative sayings.

7. Man, a composed being

7.a. Man, a composed being

For Gregory man is a double being of both body and soul and we have seen that the two components or aspects of man are regarded as contrasting ones.[141] "I am small and great, low and lofty, mortal and immortal, earthly and heavenly. The one condition I share with this world below, the other, with God, the one with the flesh, the other with the spirit."[142]

When speaking about the composition of man, Gregory uses a variety of terms with the meaning of binding together, mixing or mixture.[143] Man is a "mixture" (κρᾶμα) or a "mingling" (μῖξις) of body and soul.[144]

Man is thus understood as made up by two elements of different origin. His body is formed of earth while his soul is "a breath" of God. In spite of the distinct understanding of man as a double creation, Gregory nevertheless clearly understood him as being *one* living being. (We shall later discuss the fact though that Gregory regarded this composition as involving a risk of dissolution.) So Gregory in the text on creation in Or. 38.11 talks about Logos who having created the two kinds of natures, the spiritual and the material, further is said to produce "one living being of both"[145] and further, in the same passage, man is said to be "at the same time spirit and flesh".[146]

For Gregory the emphasis is often very strongly on the spiritual aspect of life and man. In attempting to catch his meaning though we must state that for him man is precisely the very union or mingling of spirit and matter. This and nothing else is man.

The main interest of Gregory though, as Portmann points out, does not concern the nature (das Wesen) of man or the nature of the relations of the soul to the body.[147] As Portmann appropriately formulates it, the problem for Gregory is not "*how* body and soul are joined but *why*".[148] And over this question Gregory reflected quite a lot, as we will discuss in the next chapter.

7.b. A microcosm motif

In two of the texts by Gregory on creation we find a further idea that should be observed. It concerns the understanding of man as a kind of bringing together of the two existing kinds of creations or natures.

So, in Or. 38.11, we find Gregory saying, "Mind then, and sense, in this way separated from each other, remained within their own boundaries . . . Not yet was there any mixture of both nor any mingling of these opposites . . . Now the Creator Word wanting . . . [to produce] one living being of both, I mean the invisible and visible nature, creates man. And taking the body from the already existing matter, and placing in it a breath from himself (which the Word knew to be an intelligent soul and an image of God), as a kind of second world. Great in little he placed him on earth, another angel, a mingled worshipper, fully initiated into the visible creation but only partially into the intellectual. A king of that on earth, ruled from above, earthly and heavenly, temporal and immortal, visible and intellectual, midway between greatness and lowliness, at the same time spirit and flesh."

Commenting on this text we may say that Gregory here is expressing the idea that man presents and forms a kind of representative mingling of the two kinds of created natures or worlds. It might be said to be a kind of representative union in principle, which gives the impression of man as reflecting and mirroring the whole kosmos or the world and its two "parts" or spheres in his doubleness. We may talk about a microcosm motif[149] in the teaching of Gregory, which is meant here as the idea that man in his "compositedness" reflects the doubleness of the whole "greater" cosmos and in himself unites its two kinds of natures. We even find a kind of mission or task of man related to this, as will be discussed in the next chapter, though this not is a dominant idea in the thinking of Gregory. He himself though does not generally make use of the term microcosm,[150] but in this text talks about man as "a kind of second world"[151] ($\kappa \acute{o} \sigma \mu o \varsigma$ $\delta \varepsilon \acute{v} \tau \varepsilon \rho o \varsigma$).

In the poem on the soul Gregory speaks about man in a similar way. The world-creating-Logos, having created the world, here is saying, "It has pleased me to put together a common race from both, an intelligent man between both the mortal and the immortal, both enjoying my works and a prudent initiate into heavenly things, a great might on earth, another angel of earth, praiser of my might and mind. Thus he spoke, and taking a part of the newly made earth he established my form by his immortal hands and so shared his life with it. For into it he threw the spirit which is a piece broken off the invisible deity".[152]

In this text man is talked about as "a common race from both", that is the two kinds of worlds or natures, and Logos in man unites these two kinds of natures. Commenting further on this passage we may say that Gregory, by his emphasis on the divine character of the spirit of man, "a piece broken off the invisible deity", gives the impression of not only a union of spirit and matter in man but even a bringing together of something divine with something from the earth. So Gregory even talks about the Logos who forms the figure of man of earth and shares his life with it.

The idea discussed in this paragraph is not found in many of the texts in the material. Its presence in two of the main texts where Gregory is describing the creative action of God though justifies the examination of it. Systematically speaking, we here in man find a bringing together of the two kinds of created natures, spirit and matter, which even might be understood as a kind of union of something divine with something of the earth.

In these two texts, as Portmann would direct our attention[153] we even find man talked about as having a kind of position between the two worlds, the heavenly and the earthly. A part of his position is his rank as a king or might on earth, "fully initiated into the visible creation but only partially into the intellectual".[154]

7.c. A risky compound

In a couple of texts we find Gregory expressing the idea of what might be called a kind of risk as related to composition. In Or. 28.7 f., he discusses the nature of God and the fact that God has no body. While discussing this he expresses an idea that is of interest for our theme, namely that composition is related to separation and dissolution.[155] "For composition is the origin (alt. cause, beginning) of strife, and strife of separation and separation of dissolution".[156]

In Or. 40.7 we find Gregory talking again in a similar way. "For since that to not to sin at all belongs to God and to the first and uncompounded (ἀσύνθετος) nature, for simplicity (ἁπλότης) is peaceful and without rebellion (ἀστασίαστος), and I dare to say that it even belongs to the angelic [nature], or that it is very near to this because of the nearness to God. But to sin is human and belongs to the compound (σύνθεσις) below, for composition is the origin (alt. cause, beginning) of separation,[157] [therefore] the Lord did not think he should leave his creature helpless or allow it to risk separation from him. But just as he made that which did not exist to exist, so he formed that which existed anew (ἀναπλάσσειν), a moulding more divine and higher than the first."[158]

Interpreting the texts we may say that, (1) Or. 28 talks about a risk of dissolution, separation and inner opposition as related to composition. The text might even be understood as having a moral aspect, though not necessarily. (2) In Or. 40 we find a repetition of the statement from Or. 28 "composition is the origin of separation". Here we further find a clear association and relating between composition and inclination to sin, a fact that will be further discussed in the next chapter.

Commenting further on this same idea, we may understand Gregory as meaning something that is put together of different elements involves a risk of inner opposition[159] as well of separation and dissolution.[160] The oneness of man and the unity of body and soul may thus be spoken of as a relative one.

So shall we finally conclude with the new relation between the soul and the body after the death and the resurrection of man about which Gregory speaks in a few texts. These texts do not deal very exhaustively with the theme but yet two questions should be put to them as concerns any possible understanding of them. (1) Whether Gregory did not regard the future union of the body and the soul as a higher and more close one as compared to the present one. (2) And further if he did not perhaps even mean the risk of separation and sin, that was related to the composition, in the heavenly existence will be eliminated.

At least it is possible to draw these consequences from some sayings of Gregory. In Or. 7.21 as already observed[161] the new relation of the body to the soul is described as a very closed one. The soul shall be with the body "one, both spirit and mind and god".

In Or. 38.11 God is further said to once bind man together loftier or higher, though Gregory here not is giving any further explanation as to what that will mean.

In Or. 40.7, quoted above, we find a relating of sin and composition. Gregory further talks about the Lord forming man anew, "a moulding more divine and higher than the first", as he was thinking of human weakness. Now it should be stated and stressed that the theme of this oration is baptism and not the future, heavenly life as such. But perhaps though we may interpret this "forming anew" action of baptism as an anticipation of the future life of man, and thus understand the risks of composition as being eliminated then.[162]

Chapter 3
Why is man a bodily being?

1. Introduction

In the writings of St. Gregory we find in some texts rather fascinating reflections and ideas about the significance of the mixed nature of man with the reasons for it and for his bodily nature. In this chapter we will now go further with these particular ideas.

From the preceding chapter we may say that the primary aspect of man is his divine destiny. As a spiritual being he is created for a spiritual life with God in heaven. We have even observed the attitude of Gregory to the earthly life of man. It is hard, and the bodily life of man a troublesome one (although we also found a considerably more positive attitude). A natural consequence of this attitude, and of his understanding of man as a living being created for a life with God in heaven, would now be to ask why man was given a bodily life at all and a life on earth. Gregory never expresses himself directly in this way, but we may, on the basis of his thinking, reconstruct a question like following, "If man was created for a life with God in heaven, why should he at first have to live on earth, and why was he given a body?" As previously stated, Gregory never expresses himself with exactly these words, but in some of the texts which will be discussed in this chapter, he deals directly with the question about reasons for man's mixed nature and for his body. Why did God give the body to man? It is a mystery.[1] But, by thinking of the hard sides of the bodily life and the troubles the body causes to man, Gregory is evidently looking for a reason and a significance for this. We may say that he is asking what the benefit of it is as well as of the bodily life.

As this bodily life of man is the same as his earthly life, we may even regard his ideas as a reflection about man's life on earth and the significance of it. And so, in the writings of St. Gregory, we are finding an attempt to discover the meaning and the significance of man's earthly life.

We will start the chapter with a presentation of some main texts in which we find the ideas of Gregory about the significance of the bodily or the double nature of man as well as the reasons for it, either more or less directly expressed or just hinted at. As we are finding in these texts quite a number of ideas, aspects and reflections, a preliminary comment and discussion is given immediately to each of the texts. For the sake of further discussion, a systematic summary of the ideas and aspects found in the texts is then given as the different ideas are classified in three main groups or three main lines of thought, which we find in these texts.

As the ideas expressed in the texts are closely related to Gregory's basic understanding of man and of man's original creation and situation, we must render an exhaustive presentation and discussion of Gregory's understanding of man in these respects, before we are able to go on with the further discussions of the ideas found in the main texts. In that way we will be prepared for the final discussion of Gregory's understanding of man's bodily life and the significance of his bodily nature.

Finally, something also should be said as to the character of the texts discussed in this chapter. When Gregory presents us with his reflections and ideas about man's mixed nature, we never find him giving any longer treatise or discussion of the issues considered. Instead we find a lot of short formulations with which Gregory is saying or suggesting quite a lot. In some particular texts quite a number of ideas and aspects are mentioned and accumulated. The shortness of the formulations and the treatises gives a certain suggestive character to the texts and I even think we may talk about a certain "openness" of the texts. Because of the shortness and their suggestive character, the texts invite the further associations and thoughts of the reader. I regard this "openness" as one of the great values of the writings of Gregory.

Now this character of the texts certainly presents us with some problems. Reading them we must carefully distinguish between what really is said explicitly in a text and what is to be regarded as a possible interpretation or even a possible consequence of what Gregory is saying directly.

There is a reason though for why we may build upon what is said in these texts. That reason is the inner consistency between the texts and the different ideas expressed in them as well as in the rest of the writings of St. Gregory. When we read what is said about man and his basic situation in these texts as well as in others, and try to go behind what is said, we find an inner relation and consistency between the different sayings. That is a reason for why, in spite of the lack of any longer systematic treatise on the topic of man, we may try to attempt to reconstruct the thinking of Gregory on man.

2. Some main texts

1. Or. 2.17

(Gregory in Or. 2.17 talks about the guidance of man as well as the treatment of the body and having talked about the latter so goes on with the care of souls:)

> "The other is concerned with the soul which is from God and divine, and
> partakes of the nobility above and hastens on to it, even if it is bound

together with the inferior one. Perhaps it is even because of other reasons which only God who bound them together knows and if there is someone instructed by God in such mysteries, but as far as I and those like me understand it is for the sake of two things. One, that it may inherit the glory above through struggle and wrestling with that here below, tried through that here below like gold in fire, and to obtain that which it hopes for as a prize of virtue and not only as a gift of God. And this then was the will of the highest Goodness, to make the good even our own, not only sown in our nature but cultivated by the free choice (προαίρεσις) and the motions of the free will into both directions. Two, that it may draw to itself and place the inferior one above, gradually freeing it from its grossness, in order that the soul may be to the body what God is to the soul, through itself leading (παιδαγωγεῖν) its assistant matter and intimating (οἰκειοῦν) it to God as a fellow servant."

In this text St. Gregory says that he is able to realize two reasons for the union of the soul to the body. The body in this text is just mentioned as the inferior part and no other aspects of the body are more precisely expressed or mentioned, though it's obvious that Gregory is thinking of the harder aspects of the bodily life when he talks about man's "struggle and wrestling with that here below".

Developing these two reasons Gregory mentions quite a lot of different aspects mutually connected, among which it is possible to discern certain main ideas or leading aspects. So will we turn our attention to what is said in the text and discuss the two reasons as Gregory develops them.

Reason number one: we here find a number of components and ideas but I think we are right to say that there is a main aspect expressed with the words "to make the good even our own", while the others may be regarded as a commentary on and development of this idea. What we here find expressed is the idea that the "good", and what he hopes for, is something that man acquires himself. This is further said to be accomplished through the exercise of the free will of man and through his choice. A very similar idea is even found in Or. 38. 12 where Gregory is describing the creation of man. The newly created man is in that text said to be "honoured with the free will in order that the good may belong to the choosing one no less than to him who produced the seeds [of it]".

There is further a "virtuous" as well as a "meritorious" aspect in the text. Man will get what he longs for as a "prize of virtue". We may suppose Gregory to mean that man, through his good "struggle with that here below", will reach virtue and so obtain the object of his hope as a prize and not only as a gift.

There is even a kind of "testing" aspect in the bodily life. The soul may be "tried as gold in fire".

Finally, we may observe that this acquiring of the good by man himself is related to the body and the bodily life, by a struggle with that here below.

Gregory may be supposed to mean that matter and the body, or man's bodily life on earth and in the world of matter is offering the material and the possibilities for this struggle.

Reason number two: having developed the ideas just discussed, Gregory goes on by mentioning a rather different idea as compared to the others in this text. It concerns what we may call a mission of the soul vis-a-vis the body.[2] The soul is said to have a kind of task in relation to the body. It shall bring it to God and "intimate it to God" as its fellow servant.[3] We have earlier noticed that the goal for the body as well as for the soul is the heavenly life with God, and in this text we find Gregory talking about a task for the soul in this respect.

We may further notice the kind of middle position of the soul that is expressed with the words "in order that the soul may be to the body what God is to the soul". On the whole, ontologically speaking, for Gregory the soul might be said to have a middle position, between God and the material creation, if we consider its nature. In this text we find a middle position with regard to its function, and it is evident that this function is possible just because of the ontological status of the soul.

2. Or. 14.6–7

"... [The body] that makes war when it is in good condition and grieves when war is made upon it, that I love as a fellow servant and turn away from as an enemy, that I even flee from as a fetter and honour as a joint heir. I strive to weaken it and don't know whom I may use as a cooperator for the best, knowing for what I have been made and that I ought to ascend to God through my actions.

...

... Which is this wisdom with regard to me, and which is this great mystery? Does he perhaps want that we, being a part of God and springing from above, in order not to despise our Creator exalting and elevating ourselves because of our worth, in wrestling and fight with the body always look at him, and that the weakness joined to us shall be a training ($\pi\alpha\iota\delta\alpha\gamma\omega\gamma\iota\alpha$) of our dignity? So that we may know that we at the same time are both the greatest and the lowest, earthly and heavenly, transitory and immortal, inheritors of light and fire or of darkness, whichever way we may incline to. Such is our mixture and on account of that, as it seems to me at last, in order that when we exalt ourselves because of the image, we restrain ourselves because of the earth."

In this text the body is first mentioned as a fellow servant and cooperator, (cf. Or. 2.17). Gregory says that he does not know whom to use as a cooperator for the best. Developing this he further states that he knows that he ought to ascend to God through his actions.

Here we find a kind of thinking similar to the preceding text. Man is regarded as his own agent on his way to God, and the body now might be understood as a cooperator in this.

In the second part of the text (Or. 14.7), a new idea is brought into consideration. In this passage, Gregory looks for a reason for man's bodily nature in his tendency to exalt and elevate himself. As man is created as the image of God, he may exalt himself because of this greatness and despise his Creator, but through his body he has got a kind of reminder. Probably Gregory is meaning that there is a risk that man will get puffed up because of his greatness, but having a body he will be reminded and corrected because of the lowliness of his body and the troubles his body causes.

It should be noticed that Gregory, developing this idea, does a certain amount of sliding between ideas in what he is saying and in his argumentation. As a matter of fact though, two different reasons for man's mixed nature are given in the text. They may be formulated as following.

1. Man is given a body in order to keep him from exalting himself.

2. Man is given a body as a means of correction, when he does exalt himself.

The distinction may be regarded as pointless, and the two different formulations understood as two ways of saying the same thing. But if we read the text literally, the first formulation seems to say that the body is given as a kind of preventive means or aid that will prevent man from exalting himself. Thanks to the body he will not get puffed up, which is the tendency Gregory seems to recognize in man. The second formulation on the other hand, at the end of the paragraph, seems to count with man's elevation as something that either will or might happen. The body is now noted as given to man as a mean for correction when he does exalt himself. The distinction will be discussed further on.

At any rate, the idea put forth in the text is that the body is given to man because of the tendency to which Gregory refers. The weakness of the body is said to be a kind of education (paidagogia) for man.

3. Or. 28.12

(St. Gregory, in this oration, settles the fact that man cannot apprehend God, "the Divine can't be comprehended by human intellect".[4] He then goes on to discuss the reasons for this and the cause for the setting of the bodily "darkness" between God and man.)

> "But if it is out of other reasons too they might know who are nearer God and eyewitnesses and observers of his unsearchable judgments, if there really are any of such virtue and walking in the paths of the abyss as the saying is. As far as we have comprehended however, who measure with small measures, that which is hard to understand, perhaps it is in order that that which is acquired shall not be most easily thrown away because it was so easily acquired. For usually that which is acquired

with labour is held more fast, but what is easily acquired is even most quickly let go as being possible to take hold of again. And so it is a benefit that the benefit is not easy, at least to those who are sensible. Or perhaps it is that we may not suffer the same as Lucifer, who fell and out of receiving the light fully arch our necks proudly against the allsovereign Lord and fall because of the elevation[5], a fall most pitiable of all. Or perhaps it is that the reward there may be somewhat greater for the patient industry and brilliant life of those, who have been purified here and wait patiently for what they desire. Therefore between us and God this bodily darkness is placed like the cloud of old between the Egyptians and the Hebrews. And this is perhaps [what is meant by] he made darkness his secret place, our grossness ($\pi\alpha\chi\acute{\upsilon}\tau\eta\varsigma$) through which few can see but a little."

When in this text Gregory talks about the body, he is thinking of the "darkness" of it in respect to the knowing or "seeing" of God and the hindrance of it for man's apprehending and knowledge of God. It is this incomprehensibility of God which causes his reflections about the body and the reasons for man's bodily nature. But when he develops his ideas, he is evidently even thinking of the hardships of the bodily and earthly life. In this oration he now mentions three reasons for the mixed nature of man.

1. "That which is acquired shall not be most easily thrown away because it was so easily acquired." Gregory here seems to express the conviction that man, if he did not have to work hard for it, should risk to let go again what he has acquired[6] (which we may understand as the fuller seeing of God). So therefore, the darkness of the body has been put between God and man. The idea here seems to be that man, if he directly and immediately had been put into the full seeing of God might have let this "benefit" go because it was so easily acquired. This is according to the rule that man values more highly that for which he has to work. According to this idea, man's bodily life may be regarded as a kind of preventive measure to rescue man from too risky a fate.

2. Even in the second argument the body is given a kind of preventive meaning and significance. The idea is that man shall be hindered and protected from the kind of fate that Lucifer suffered. What does this saying mean? Gregory seems to mean that man, if from the beginning he had received the light fully, he might have exalted himself like Lucifer and suffered the same kind of fall that Lucifer did. So therefore, from the beginning, thanks to the body and darkness of it put between man and God, man did not receive the light fully and did not have the ability of full "seeing" or contemplation of God (cf. Or. 38.11−12). We will meet this rather special idea of Gregory in another of the texts and discuss the meaning of it again later in this chapter.

What might be said here is that Gregory seems to recognize the risk of a fall in man. We may even say that he recognizes the risk of pride and self-elevation, and that he looks for a preventive and protective meaning in the grossness of the body in relation to this risk.

3. As the third reason, Gregory may think that the desired life will be a reward for the life of those who have been long suffering here. We come here upon the same "meritorious" and even "virtuous" aspect that we met in the first of the texts. Further a "purifying" aspect is mentioned in this text.

It shall be noticed that common to all the argumentation is the idea that there is a benefit for man in the "darkness" of the body. In the third reason, this benefit is even related to the hardship of the body and the bodily life.

4. Or. 38.11
(Gregory describes God's creation of man as a mixed being.)

> "And taking the body from the already existing matter, and placing in it a breath from himself (which the Word knew to be an intelligent soul and an image of God), as a kind of second world. Great in little, he placed him on the earth, another angel, a mingled worshipper, fully initiated into the visible creation but only partially into the intellectual. A king of that on earth, ruled from above, earthly and heavenly, temporal and immortal, visible and intellectual, midway between greatness and lowliness, at the same time spirit and flesh, spirit because of the grace, flesh because of the pride. The one that he might continue to live and to give honour to his benefactor. The other that he might suffer and suffering be reminded and corrected, if he became proud of his greatness."

In this text we find first what we may call a microcosm motif. Man being a mixture of the natures, the intelligible and the material is said to be a kind of "second world". His relation to the material world is expressed with the words "king of that on earth" and "fully initiated into the visible creation" and he is described as being given a kind of middle position between God and the material world, at the same time related to both.

Further we again find the idea about man's pride. Gregory here expresses the opinion that man is given a body as a means of correction or of chastiment if he becomes proud of his greatness as a spiritual being. We find two ideas in the text.

a) The risk of man's pride (éparsis).

b) The pedagogical or corrective significance of the body.

5. PD 4.84 f.

> "In order that creation coming near God and longing for godlike glory should not lose (alt. destroy, ὀλλύναι) light and glory, (For the best thing is to bear limitation, but intemperance is the worse), therefore the high Logos being kindly minded towards those who should become, threw all the light surrounding the throne away from the Trinity, and the mortal

nature away from the angelic troops. The angelic [nature] not being far away as ministers, but ours even very much far away, since we descend from earth mixed with deity, but a simple nature is better."

This text might be compared to Or. 28.12 discussed above. Here, even in the beginning of the passage, we come upon something that might be called a kind of "preventative measure", though the idea in this text is not as developped as in Or. 28.12 "In order that creation, coming near God and longing for godlike glory, should not lose light and glory", something now is happening and a kind of arrangement may be said to be made. Logos, being kindly minded towards those who should become or be created, threw them away from God. How shall that now be understood and interpreted? As I read the text I understand it as a kind of parallel to that of Or. 28.12. In order that the newly made creation "longing for godlike glory should not lose light and glory" (that is to my understanding, suffering a fall) it is thrown away from God, or we may say put at a distance from Him. The angelic world is placed rather near God, whereas the human beings on the contrary are placed at a greater distance from Him, "very much far away".

If to start with, we now look to man, the mortal nature, the passage might be understood to talk about a preventive measure by which man is put at a distance, far from God, in order not to suffer a fall and "loose light and glory".

Now, before going on, it should be stated that the text provides us with some difficulties. (For an alternative, though hardly probable translation, see note 7.) In Or. 28.12 we came upon a kind of preventive arrangement with regard to man in order that man, different from Lucifer and contrary to him, should not suffer the same fate as he did. According to Or. 28.12, man should be prevented from having a fall like Lucifer's. But in this text, we now meet a contrary arrangement which even seems to include the angels. The preventive measure even includes them.

It should be further observed as a matter of fact, that Gregory, already earlier in this poem, has been talking about Satan "losing (or destroying) light and glory through his proud confidence", using the same terms as in our passage here.[8] For the interpretation of this text I see two possibilities. a) Either Gregory means that God, in making the creation, provided an arrangement to rescue the angels as well as the human beings from "losing light and glory", but in the case of Lucifer this failed. b) An other alternative might be that Gregory here is doing a kind of sliding between thoughts. Talking about "creation" ($\kappa\tau i\sigma\iota\varsigma$) in the beginning of the passage he is perhaps just thinking about man who in order not to "lose light and glory" is placed at a distance far away from God. But developing this idea he even mentions the angels put at a relative distance from God.

As it concerns man, I understand Gregory to mean that Logos or the Word, in order to prevent the new created man from a kind of fall, puts him at a distance far away from God. And further, this distance, and this is a main point in the interpretation of the text, is said to be due to the bodily stature of man. We are far away from God "since we descend from earth mixed with deity". And so we even in this passage find a kind of preventive arrangement related to the body of man and to his double and composed nature.

It has earlier been noted that Gregory evidently was thinking of man and the earth as being at a distance from God in contrast to the nearness of the angelic world to God.[9] So I understand him to be thinking of the material creation as being at a kind of distance from God.[10] In this text man is now said to be far away from God as he is a bodily or material being. So we may understand Gregory as meaning that man, just because of his bodily and composed nature, is placed at a distance from God, and this distance, as previously noted, has a kind of preventive or protective function. This text is the only one in which I have found, a) the idea directly and explicitly expressed that man, thanks to his body, is placed at a distance from God, and further b) that this distance performs a preventive function. These ideas fit very well though with the others that will be discussed in this chapter. They will be presupposed as a part of the thinking of Gregory in the continuing discussion, and in the interpretation of his thinking which will be made here.

6. PD 8.57 f.
(The Word having created the world now creates man:)

> "But as all this was the world, both earth and heaven and sea, he sought for someone acquainted with the wisdom, mother of all, and a godfear-ing king for that on earth and said this; Already pure and everliving ser-vants, holy minds inhabit the wide heaven, noble angels, hymners who celebrate my everlasting fame. But the earth yet exults in thoughtless life (alt: but the earth yet honours me by thoughtless life[11]). It has pleased me to put together a common race from both, an intelligent man between both the mortal and the immortal, both enjoying my works and a pru-dent initiate in heavenly things. A great might on earth, another angel of earth, praiser of my might and mind. Thus he spoke and taking a part of the newly made earth he established my form by his immortal hands and so shared his life with it."

In this text we come upon some different ideas concerning man and his tasks and functions which have been rather sparsely represented in the previous texts. Briefly, man is talked about as a race blended from two natures or worlds and is further understood as having a function vis-à-vis the earth, i.e. being a king, as well as vis-à-vis God, as a praiser of him and as someone able to enjoy his works.

Man is further spoken of as having a kind of middle position. This is only ex-plicitly referred to at one occasion, but Gregory's way of describing man as an "angel of earth" and a king or might on earth gives a certain impression of both his position and function. He is more than a purely earthly being. We may understand the function of man, as described in the text, as due to his double nature and the middle position this gives him. We may further see him as participating in both the material and the spiritual reality. And so, God has "an angel on earth" as well as a king for it.

In Or. 38.11 Gregory talks about "sense" or the material creation as a silent praiser of God. Following our alternative reading of this text we here find the idea that God, thanks to man, is now praised even on the earth by spiritual beings.[12]

3. Three main lines of thought

In the texts which have just been discussed we have met quite a number of various reflections and aspects. It is evident that when Gregory looked for a reason for man's bodily nature, he searched for it in several different directions. When we look at the texts we find certain ideas dominating some of the texts while Gregory stresses different aspects in others. In spite of the variety of reflections and ideas, I think it now is possible to discern certain leading ideas in the texts, and it is evident that when Gregory looked for the significance of the body and the mixed nature of man, he followed some different lines of thought. Perhaps we may say that he had some different ideas or hypotheses which he tests. Sometimes they are expressed just as statements and facts, but sometimes they have more the character of suggestive ideas or theses and I do not believe this is merely a question of rhetoric or rhetorical style. It is evident that Gregory formulated the question of the reasons for man's double nature and tried to find some sensible answers to it (these are of course based upon his assumptions and his convictions about the nature of man and his destiny).

When we look at what Gregory is saying in the texts I think we may discern three different lines of thought or three areas within which Gregory is developing his ideas and reflections. Particularly the first two of these, as they are numbered below, are closely connected to each other, as we will discuss further on. I would tend to think we are right in saying that we here find several lines of thinking and that they have to be separated for us to be able to see and understand what Gregory really is saying. Thus we may discern the following three main aspects.

1. The tendency of man to sin and fall

In several of the texts the ideas that Gregory is discussing are related to what might be called the tendency of man to sin and fall. As a matter of fact, this aspect is the one that occurs most often as compared to the others and it is evidently a dominant motif in the thinking of Gregory. (Or. 14.7, 28.12, 38.11 and PD 4.84) Man is given a body because of his tendency to elevate himself.

A related idea is the one in Or. 28.12 where Gregory talks about the risk of man too easily letting go of the "possession" if it was too easily acquired.

2. Man may himself acquire "the good" and the life with God

A different kind of idea is the one we met in Or. 2.17 and which we tried to characterize with the words that the good and what man hopes for is something that he should acquire himself. A similar aspect of the life of man is expressed in Or. 14.6 where Gregory says that he knows for what end he has been made and that he ought "to ascend to God through actions". A kindred aspect is even found in Or. 28.12 (reason number three).

3. A microcosm motif

Rather different from the two first aspects is the third one which I think may be pointed out in the texts. Summarizing the ideas here, we may talk about a microcosm motif in the theology of Gregory, that is an understanding of man as summing up the two kinds of created natures in his mixed being. Further related to this is a certain understanding of his role and function. This kind of thinking we find more or less fully expressed in Or. 2.17, 38.11 and PD 8.57ff.

4. The original state of man, the fall and man's tendency toward sin and fall

The ideas and reflections which we have found in the texts above (and among which we have just discerned three main aspects) show Gregory's basic understanding of man, his situation and the significance of his life and its conditions. Generalizing, we may say that what we have met are reflections about the basic data and facts concerning the life of man. For the further discussions of these texts it is now necessary to start an examination of Gregory's general understanding of the basic and original situation of man, since his theology in this respect is closely related to the ideas found in our texts. We will therefore now go on with Gregory's understanding of the primordial state of man and his original creation and situation. From the beginning, man, for Gregory, was not a fully mature being and we shall examine his understanding of this "infancy" of man. Further, as we have seen, Gregory speaks in regard to the inclination of man to sin and fall, and this also has to be discussed. Gregory's understanding concerning the fall of man is rather complicated, and it has also been interpreted somewhat differently in the literature. Thus, we have to deal rather exhaustively with his thinking in this respect before we then will be able to return to his understanding of the bodily nature and life of man.

5. The original "infancy" of Adam

Gregory is a theologian in whose thinking we find the well known idea from Irenaeus about the original infancy of the first man, Adam. Gregory thus does not teach the original perfection of man. We may say that he talks about the first man as being in a state of immaturity in several aspects. That means that we may interpret him as not understanding the first life of man in "paradise" as identical to the later life in heaven toward which man's life tends. Summarizing, we may describe Gregory's idea of the first man as following.

Adam, the first man, was from the beginning not yet in full maturity.[13] He had not received the "light" fully, which means that he had not yet a full share of the divine light[14] and was still not mature or prepared for theoria, the contemplation of God.[15]

Reading Genesis 2:17, Gregory in Or. 38.12 makes a certain interpretation of the tree of knowledge in paradise,[16] the tree of whose fruit man should not partake, and understands it as theoria, contemplation. From the beginning, man should not have had access to this tree, and his original sin and transgression was accordingly that he ate too early from it.[17] In Or. 38.12 Gregory says regarding this tree of knowledge, "But it would have been good if partaken of at the proper time, for the tree was, according to my theory, contemplation, upon which it is only safe for those who are in a more perfect condition to enter, but which is not good for those who are yet more simple and greedy in their appetite."

Thus, from the beginning, man had only a partial share of the divine light, but Gregory evidently reckoned that eventually man should reach the "seeing" of God.[18] Reading what Gregory is saying about the primordial state of man, we now find some different features that should be mentioned and which are parts of his picture of this state of imperfection or "not-yet-perfection" as we may call it.

1) Adam was immature or childish. As a matter of fact Gregory himself generally doesn't use the word "child" for Adam. In PD 8.111 he does speak though about the "childish" ones.

2) Adam did not have a full share of the light. That is, he couldn't fully "see" or contemplate God. If we now compare this to what was said earlier about the function of the body, as a darkness and hindrance for man's knowing of God, it is likely that Gregory regarded the body and man's double nature as the fact that conditioned his only partial share of the "light".[19] The body was a kind of veil or grossness that kept man back from the full seeing of God.

3) The primordial man was not allowed to eat from the tree of knowledge, which meant that he should keep back from theoria. In the discussions of the texts above we have met the idea that man, in order not to suffer a great fall like Lucifer's, from the beginning was not given the ability for the full "seeing" of God.[20] With this idea of Gregory in mind, it is measure on behalf of man "that

we may not suffer the same as Lucifer who fell, and out of having received the light fully arch our necks proudly against the all-sovereign Lord and fall because of the elevation, a fall most pitiable of all."[21] We may understand Gregory as meaning that if man had, from the beginning, received the light fully, he might have run a risk of a fall, through self-exaltation.

4) Finally, there is another aspect of the original situation of man, as Gregory speaks of it, that should be observed. We might call it a moral-existential aspect. It will be discussed further when we deal with the fall of man, but it needs to be mentioned already at this point as a part of the view of the primordial state of man.

At some occasions, when Gregory talks about the creation of man, he talks about him as able to move in either of two directions, good or evil. Thus in *PD* 8.101 f, he says that God, when he had created man put him in paradise "wavering in balance seeing in which direction he should incline", and in *PD* 9.82 f. he talks about man as "mutable" or "liable to moral lapse" and says that God didn't created me as god, but made me "inclining both ways and mutable".[22]

What Gregory is talking about here might be understood in two somewhat different ways. In the quoted texts, he talks about man as someone who might move in either of two directions morally.

a) This moral "mobility" might now be understood as a kind of ambiguity or ambivalence of man and a kind of weakness. In the later text (*PD* 9.82 ff.) it is evident that Gregory is thinking of the "mutability" of man as a moral weakness. He is "liable to moral lapse".

b) But there is even another possibility in the reading of the texts, at least the first one (*PD* 8.101 f.), and another way of interpretation for which the text is open. This might be labelled a "personal" one. With his formulation, especially in the first of the texts, St. Gregory, as I understand him, not only gives the impression of man as an ambiguous being, but of someone who is facing two possibilities. From this point of view, it is possible to read the text(s) as a description of man, from the beginning a being placed before two possibilities, good or evil. Gregory doesn't develop his ideas any further in the texts, but it is fully possible to understand his formulations not only as a description of the weakness of man but as an account of the actual situation which, from the beginning, man was a part of as a created, free, spiritual being.

The first text is, however, even open for a further interpretation. We may thus understand man as being, from the beginning, at a point of departure and at the point of departure there is the possibility to move in either of two directions. We may further understand man as facing a decision as to which inclination he will choose. A possible consequence of this is to understand the first man as someone who had yet not chosen his attitude. This understanding of the basic situation of man will be discussed further in the later part of this chapter, but I want to show the kind of implications that might be drawn from the formulation of Gregory and even to which his theology is open, as well as the consequences that might be drawn from what he is saying.

Thus Gregory might be understood in two somewhat different ways, as has just been discussed. As to the original weakness of man we even find this aspect in the text from Or. 38.12, which is quoted above. On the whole Gregory seems to have recognized a kind of moral weakness in the original man, as we will discuss in the next section which deals with the fall of man.

Thus far is Gregory's thinking about the primordial situation of man as a state of immaturity and not yet perfection. Closely related to this, of course, is Gregory's understanding of the fall of man and his original transgression and the kind of conditions and situation that led to it, and we will now go on to Gregory's thinking concerning these matters.

6. The fall of man

6.a. Introduction

When Gregory is looking for a reason for the bodily nature of man he sometimes, as we have seen, relates it to an original tendency of man to sin and fall. Now Gregory's thinking on this tendency of man as well as his thinking on the actual fall of man is rather complicated, as has previously been mentioned. A part of this is due to the fact that Gregory generally talks about the fall in what might be called a "spiritual" way, as a spiritual or personal event. On the other hand, on some occasions he relates the sin of man to his composite nature and stresses the compounded nature of man as a fact that gives account for his tendency to sin. All this requires a rather exhaustive preliminary discussion.

As is the case in the most of the theology of St. Gregory, we don't find any systematic treatise on this question or any longer discussions of the question. That means that we have to look for his thinking in quite a number of texts where the fall of man is at times talked about more explicitly and at other times just mentioned in connection with other issues. In spite of the lack of any longer systematic treatise, I think it is possible to discern Gregory's thinking in this point as well as his understanding of man's primordial situation and position.

When we read the texts we discover quite a number of aspects to them, some of them rather different from each other. One of the problems with the reading of the texts is related to understanding these aspects and their interrelatedness as well as which of them should be understood as primary and secondary emphases respectively.

Gregory has been understood in different ways on this point in the existing literature, and the authors observe different aspects of those mentioned. As my own understanding of Gregory differs from the one suggested by some of these authors, a discussion with the literature will be necessary in this chapter. I find it important that Gregory's thinking on this point really be examined in all its aspects. It not only concerns the primordial state of the "first" human being and what once happened, but even concerns his understanding of man as such and the existential position of man.

As concerning the method of reading the texts, I think it is of importance not only to see what is actually explicitly stated, but even to look to the categories which Gregory is using when he is talking about the fall of man and his tendency to sin. This is of importance for a proper balancing of the different aspects, as a too literal reading of certain texts otherwise would lead to what I regard as a definite misunderstanding of Gregory's views.

6.b. Man's tendency to pride and self-elevation against God

We will start with the aspect of the fall which we have already met, man's tendency to pride and self-elevation or rebellion against God. In several texts Gregory speaks about this tendency of man and the risk related to it.[23] The ground for this feared elevation of man is his greatness as being created in the image of God. Because of this there is a risk that he might become too proud of this, his greatness, and elevate himself over against God because of his rank. Reading the texts gives one the impression of a kind of presumptious pride of man, or perhaps we may say vain hybris. Man might be seized by a dangerous desire for "godlike glory" and "lose light and glory".[24]

We might observe that Gregory, on some occasions, is talking about the fall of Lucifer and using the same kind of terms. I mention this at this point as it is of some importance for the remainder of the discussion. In Or. 28.12 the risk of a fall of man is compared to the actual fall of Lucifer, and in Or. 38.9 Lucifer's fall is said to be caused by his pride (éparsis),[25] which is the term that Gregory uses in Or. 38.11 for this tendency of man.[26]

In *PD* 4.84f Gregory is saying that creation should be prevented from "loosing light and glory". As already discussed, earlier in the same poem, he has spoken about Satan with the same terms, as one who "looses light and glory through his proud confidence".[27]

6.c. The fall that should be avoided

Now, before going on with the discussion, we have to make a certain distinction in order to understand Gregory's rather complicated and special thinking about man on this point. Gregory, particularly when he is talking about this tendency of man, as I understand him, seems to distinguish between two "kinds" or "types" of fall: 1) the kind of fall that Lucifer or Satan suffered, who lived in the nearness of God in the heavenly sphere, but fell out of pride and became "darkness",[28] "a fall most pitiable of all"[29] and, 2) the fall of Adam.

The thinking of Gregory may be reconstructed as following. Before man was created, the world of the angels came into being, a world in the nearness of God. Within this world the fall of Lucifer took place. We may understand Gregory to understand this fall as a terrible one, the fall of a heavenly being living in the nearness to God.[30]

Gregory now seems to mean that God, when he created man, wanted to protect man from this terrible kind of fall and therefore made some arrangements in order to avoid or prevent it.[31] Therefore, man, from the beginning, was not given the full light as Lucifer,[32] nor was he put into the nearness of God. On the contrary, he was placed at a distance from God.[33]

We may say that Gregory seems to have realized that if man, from the beginning, had been put in the nearness of God, he might have suffered a fall as terrible as Lucifer's. I think we may ascribe to him the idea or insight that man certainly was a being created for a spiritual life in the nearness of God, but that from the beginning he might not endure this risky nearness.

So, this risky situation and a very disastrous fall were to be avoided. I even think that we must suppose that Gregory meant that indeed this fall truly was avoided. Thus, the actual fall of the first man, Adam, was consequently a less dangerous and terrible one, though it certainly was a fall. How could that be accomplished? It is here that Gregory looks for one of the reasons for man's double nature and for his body. Thanks to the body, man is protected from the nearness of God and placed at a distance from him.

6.d. The actual fall of Adam

In this reading of Gregory, we have come to distinguish between two kinds of falls, on the one hand, the terrible kind of fall that man was protected from, and on the other hand, the actual fall of Adam. How then does Gregory speak about Adam's actual fall? To understand this we must take into consideration not only what Gregory directly and explicitly states about the fall of the first man, but even how he looks upon the primordial state of the first man, his situation, and his status.

As we have noted, Gregory describes Adam as a kind of immature being, who lived in a condition of immaturity and was yet not given the full light of God. That is to say, he was not allowed to eat of the tree of knowledge, which Gregory in Or. 38.12 understand as theoria, contemplation. We have above described and discussed the existential and moral aspect of the primordial situation of man. We then observed that Gregory, in some of the texts, describes the first man as a being with a capacity or possibility to move into two directions, good or evil. Discussing this, we even noticed a double aspect to this condition, which is both regarded as a kind of weakness of man and as a more personal aspect. In a similar way in Or. 38.12, Gregory describes Adam as a being endowed with a free will. "This being he placed in paradise . . . having honoured him with the free will in order the good may belong to the choosing one no less than to him who produced the seeds [of it]". He further says that God gave Adam a law as a material for his free will.

In all of these aspects, the primordial situation of man must be taken into consideration when we look to Gregory's understanding of the fall. Summarizing them we may mention: the immaturity of Adam and the certain instability or weakness of him, further, his lack of the full divine light, the prohibition to eat from the tree of knowledge (theoria), and finally, his ability to move into different directions and his endowment with free will.

What now is the sin of Adam and the transgression that led to the fall and the banishing of man from the paradise? According to Gregory, the sin of Adam was that he too early tasted of the fruit of the tree of knowledge.[34] That is to say, Adam rushed too quickly into the tasting of the tree, an experience for which he was not ready. In doing this he transgressed the commandment and the prohibition of God. As the commandment was said to be a kind of material for his free will,[35] this disobedience of Adam[36] must be understood as a fault and transgression of his free will. And perhaps we may even say a kind of misuse of the free will, and the ability to move morally.

6.e. The freedom of man

Before going on with the discussion, we shall stop for a while at the freedom of man and give our attention to the view of Gregory in this respect. It is of importance for the understanding of the fall of man as well as for the continuing discussion concerning the main issue of this chapter, the significance of the body and the purpose of man's composite nature.

Adam is thus understood as a being with a free will,[37] and we have met Gregory's reflections on the choice of man.[38]

We must say that on the whole, Gregory highly values the freedom of man and emphasizes the worth of that which is the result of a free choice and not of force. We have noticed that the first, primordial man for him is a being with a kind of moral mobility and a free will. Gregory, on several occasions, stresses the importance of free choice. Only that which is the result of a free choice is really durable, and thus Gregory recommends persuasion instead of force.[39] In Or. 2.15, where one of the themes of the oration is the care of souls, Gregory thus states, "For that which is involuntary, apart from its being the result of oppression, is neither praiseworthy nor durable. For that which is forced, like a plant violently drawn aside by our hands, when set free, returns to what it was before, but that which is the result of choice is both most legitimate and firm for it is preserved by the bond of good will."[40] In another text, where celibacy is a theme, Gregory contrasts those who are "enuchs by nature" to those who "have made themselves eunuchs for the sake of the kingdom of God", that is by choice (proairesis), and says "for the good, which is by nature is not approved, but that which is by choice is laudable".[41]

I want to stress this attitude of Gregory toward the freedom of man as it certainly is part of his basic attitude toward man and of his apprehension of man. We will return to this attitude further on when we deal with his understanding of the meaning of man's bodily and earthly life.

6.f. The fall of Adam, a less disastrous one?

We have distinguished the actual fall of Adam from the terrible Lucifer-like fall that needs to be avoided. Does Gregory really mean that the actual fall of Adam was a less disastrous one, a "smaller" kind of fall? It should be clearly noted that Gregory never says this explicitly, but as an open consequence of his idea about the Lucifer-like fall that should be avoided, I think it is fair to Gregory to come to such conclusions.

This is even the attitude of H. Althaus, who thoroughly discusses this matter.[42] Althaus, when he considers the fall of Adam, observes and stresses two aspects, namely the childish character of Adam and the fact that his transgression was caused by the deceit of the Devil.[43] Althaus asserts that Gregory's teaching on the primordial state of man is rather rudimentary.[44] Because of that it causes difficulties when we want to get a proper understanding of the role of Adam and if he "really had a full knowledge of what he did".[45] That is, Althaus questions the responsibility of Adam, but states that Gregory really maintains a full responsibility of the first man. Saying this though, Althaus stresses the two aspects just mentioned (Adam's infancy and the role of Satan) and regards them as extenuating circumstances. It is at this point that I want to call the opinion of Althaus into question to a certain degree. I think he emphasizes too strongly the infancy of Adam, thus lessening the importance of the fall in too great a degree.[46]

As already said Gregory never explicitly refers to the infancy of Adam when he comments upon his fall. Nevertheless, Adam's immaturity is a part of the complete picture and contributes to impression and understanding of the reader. Accordingly, Althaus is probably quite right when he takes the immaturity of Adam into consideration, but I think he goes a bit too far in drawing his conclusions. This attitude of Althaus is probably a consequence of another one of his positions, namely, his tendency to lessen the spiritual aspect of the fall of man, but the discussion of this shall wait until the end of this section.

What has been said so far might give the impression that the whole purpose of the "arrangement" described above is to rescue man from a truly great and terrible fall by an arrangement that makes the fall that might come a less disastrous one. The greater fall is changed to a lesser one. But I don't think this is the whole truth.

One of the purposes of man's life on earth, as I understand Gregory, is not only to change the greater risked fall to a lesser one, but to send man to a life in which his character might be strengthened and in which he might himself choose the "good" by a free choice.[47] As I understand Gregory it is precisely through this that the greater fall is avoided, and herein lies one of the points in the anthropology of Gregory as I see it. One of the reasons for the life on earth was that the risk of a great fall should be avoided. But, we may ask at this point, if there is any guarantee that man, once he has reached the life of God, will not suffer a fall anyway. In the theology of Gregory we find an implied answer to this question, something that might be called the "strengthening" of the character of man on earth and his free choice, and his own acquiring of the good.

6.g. The personal and spiritual character of the fall

Some of the literature[48] has questioned the existence of what we may call both the personal and the spiritual character of the fall of man. But, I want to stress both these aspects in Gregory's way of speaking.

In the beginning of this passage, we started the discussion with man's tendency to pride and to self-elevation against God. These certainly must be said to be personal categories and a way of talking about man in personal terms. We have so far mainly discussed this tendency of man in relation to the "great", disastrous fall, that should be avoided. It is evident though that Gregory even related this to the actual fall of Adam. In some of the texts which are discussed in this chapter (Or. 14.7 and 38.11), man is said to have been given a body as a means of chastening, if and when he should become proud over his greatness. A conclusion from these texts must be that Gregory suggests that God, in his foresight, reckoned with this possibility when he created man.[49] That is to say, the aspect of pride and elevation is even related to the actual fall.

This fall is even talked about as an act of disobedience,[50] which also must be said to be a personal aspect.

Further, we must stress the freedom of man and Adam as a free agent, and what I have called his moral mobility, an ability to move into different directions morally.

As evidence for a spiritual understanding of the fall of Adam even some texts should be mentioned where Gregory directly talks about the fall as a fall of the mind and soul respectively, that is man's highest faculty and spiritual aspect. In Ep. 101, col. 188, Gregory talks about the incarnation of Christ and his bearing of even a mind. He states that Christ needed "a mind because of the mind, which not only fell in Adam, but was the first to be affected." In the same way, Gregory talks about the incarnation in Or. 2 and talks about the flesh and soul of Christ, "the soul because of the soul that was disobedient, the flesh because of the flesh that assisted and was condemned with it."[51]

6.h. The composite nature of man as cause for his sin

We have thus far discussed the spiritual or personal aspect of the fall. However Gregory sometimes talks about the tendency to sin and the causes for man's sinfulness in a different way. That also requires observation and discussion. What is here brought into consideration is the composite nature of man.

In Or. 40.7 Gregory talks about the tendency toward sin and states that only God is capable of total sinlessness. In doing this he relates this tendency of man to his composite nature. "For since that not to sin at all belongs to God and to the first and uncompounded nature, for simplicity is peaceful and without rebellion, and I dare to say that it even belongs to the angelic [nature], or that it is very near to this because of the nearness to God. But to sin is human and belongs to the compound below, for composition is the origin of separation."[52]

What Gregory here says is that man, because of his compositedness and the consequent risk of dissolution and separation, is exposed to sin and that total sinlessness because of his nature is an impossibility for him. Only God transcends this risk of sin because of his simplicity, and we may suppose that Gregory here is thinking of the pure spiritual character of God and his nature.

We may here discern two different aspects in the text. 1) The relation of sinfulness to the compositedness of man. 2) The statement of Gregory that only God is superior to sin.[53] These two aspects don't necessarily have to be connected to each other, though it is evident that Gregory in this text relates them.

We will start the discussion with the first of the two aspects. This relationship between sin and the composite nature is even found in some other texts, although this text (Or. 40.7) is the only one where Gregory so openly expresses this idea. In Or. 28.7 he states, "For composition is the origin of strife and strife of separation and separation of dissolution".[54] We may say that Gregory here gives expression to the law or rule that something that is a composition and is thus made out of several components, is exposed to a risk of inner conflict and disharmony. How should this idea of Gregory be understood? It is evident that he is not aiming at an assumed evilness of the body as such. We may not understand him as equating sin and corporality. It is more a question of the doubleness of man as the idea is expressed in the texts thus far related.

We may compare this to what Gregory says about the angels. These are said to be difficult to move into the direction of evil,[55] though Gregory, in Or. 38, says that he would have liked to think of them as incapable of being moved.[56] Further, in some texts, Gregory expresses a certain difficulty or uncertainty as to the nature of the angels and ascribes to them some degree of materiality or corporality.[57] It is now likely that Gregory related the following two facts, though he never directly does this in any of the texts:[58] a) the possibility of sin in the angels, b) their corporality. A relating of sinfullness and corporality which might be compared to the relating of sinfulness and compositedness above.

It thus seems that Gregory had to relate sin to compositedness, and perhaps we should even say to corporality and materiality as such. We may understand him to mean that only God is totally simple in his nature and totally above sin as expressed in the passage from Or. 40.7 quoted above.

We may ask why Gregory did this relating. Was it necessary for him to think of sin in terms of materiality and corporality, for example the body being the place of the passions? This is at least how Althaus understands him.[59] Or, is it rather a question of compositedness as such and the inherent risk of inner conflict and separation? Is it an equating of lack of simplicity to instability and the corresponding idea that only that which is totally simple is totally stable and thus incapable of evil?

6.i. The weakness of man

On the whole, we have seen that Gregory looks at the primordial man as afflicted with a kind of weakness, and we will now at last come to this aspect of the fall. When we earlier in this chapter dealt with the infancy of Adam, we noticed some texts where Gregory expresses this weakness. In *PD* 9.82f Gregory talks about the instability and moral mobility of man, and in Or. 38. 12 he also talks about Adam in a manner that gives the impression of a moral instability.[60]

In the texts quoted in the beginning of this chapter, there is even a hint of a similar understanding of man. In Or. 2.17 and 28.12, when Gregory looks for a reason for the bodily nature of man, he mentions a kind of aspect of testing and purifying. Perhaps by wrestling with this below and through being "tried as gold in fire", man shall gain the life with God.[61] Behind this we may find the idea that man because of a kind of primordial weakness needed to be strengthened in his character through his life on earth. In Or. 28.12, we find another idea which presupposes a primordial instability in man. Here Gregory mentions the risk that man, if he had directly got the thing he desired and had not valued it fully enough, might have let it go again.

In Or. 40.7 quoted above, we met the statement that only God is superior to sin (aspect number two), a saying that we even find in other texts.[62] At last Gregory's reflections on composition, which we have discussed above, should be mentioned here, as composition implies a certain weakness.

We may say that Gregory generally recognized that the first man was afflicted by a kind of weakness. If we now also take his idea of the great, dangerous fall that should be avoided into consideration, I think we may say that Gregory realized a risk and a danger with the existence of man as such. As soon as man was created, the risk of a fall was a possibility. And it is further possible to say that Gregory realized a risk of a fall and an instability of everything created.[63] Is it possible to create someone "perfect" from the beginning and in moral stability? Indirectly, the theology of Gregory denies that.

We may discuss what caused Gregory to think in this direction. As a background for his thinking, I think we are obliged to regard the wrestling with the problem of theodicy, which occupied the thinking of the ancients, both Christian and non-Christian alike.

We may even suppose that the thinking of Origen had its influence on Gregory in this respect. Gregory seems to belong to those who repudiated the famous idea of Origen about the prehistoric existence of the souls and their prehistoric fall in a spiritual world and existence.[64] But I think we are right to discern a strong influence of this idea in the thinking of Gregory, though "used" in quite a different way. We may say that Origen's idea of the prehistoric fall in the spiritual world got Gregory to think about the risk of such a fall. He realizes that, if man had been put in the nearness of God, he might have suffered a greater fall, as we have discussed above, and perhaps we are right to think that Origen inspired Gregory to think along such lines. Gregory's answer to this problem, as I understand him, is found in his idea that in order for man to be protected from the kind of fall that Origen believes to have happened (but Gregory does not believe happened), he was created as a bodily being with all its consequences, as previously discussed.

6.k. The fall of man. Summary

When summarizing Gregory's view of the fall I think we at the same time have to give attention to several aspects. The fall certainly was an action of man as a free agent and a spiritual event. But we even must suppose Gregory to have understood it as a result of a certain weakness of man and instability. This instability does not only concern the infancy of Adam. If that were the case, it would have been enough to create him "perfect" from the beginning. But Gregory realized that even then he would have run the risk of a fall. So we may say that Gregory considered the risk of a fall as an inevitable aspect of the created existence as such. We may ascribe to him the insight that as soon as something, or rather someone, is created there is a risk of a fall into sin. When we later continue the discussion of the bodily life of man, we shall see how Gregory takes this risk in consideration. It is fascinating to see how he reflects about the way in which this risk of creation might be overcome and abolished.

We have seen that Gregory even brings the composite nature of man in consideration, and we have discussed possible ways to understand his thinking about this issue. One of the aspects of the composite nature of man is according to Gregory its inherent risk of inner conflict and separation. We may now see this as an aspect of the weakness of man, which contributed to the fall and even made it possible.

6.1. The Gregory-literature on his understanding of the fall

As we have noticed there are quite a number of aspects in Gregory's understanding of the fall of man and his original tendency to sin. These aspects also have been differently understood and emphasized by the different authors. We shall now continue with a discussion of these different ways of reading Gregory.

By way of introduction, we may say that the difference concerns the understanding of the fall as a spiritual event or as caused by the composite nature of man respectively.

By way of simplification, we may say that one of the authors, Otis, only stresses the latter aspect, thus neglecting and even denying the spiritual one. Two of them, Althaus and Portmann, acknowledge the spiritual aspect though put the main accent on the "composited-ness" (Althaus though is not quite consistent), while the others, Spidlík, Plagnieux and Winslow, stress the spiritual one. We shall start the discussion with the two of the authors who deal more exhaustively with the question of the fall of Adam and the original possibility of sin and transgression.

Althaus is the one who most exhaustively deals with the question of the fall of man and its causes. He observes most of the aspects mentioned above, even the very specific idea of Gregory concerning the greater fall that should be avoided.[65] But in doing this, he talks with a certain inconsistency.

We may say that we find two lines of thought in Althaus' understanding of Gregory. (1) On the one hand Althaus regards the sinfulness of man and his fall as something caused by the composite nature of man and his bodily character.[66] His discussion shall not be reiterated in detail, but one of his main points is that the spirit of man in the fall was conquered by the flesh and its passions, and enslaved by it.[67] What I mainly want to call into question here is the way Althaus is talking about the spirit of man and its role and part in the fall. Althaus gives the impression that the spirit was a victim of the body, thus diminishing its share and response for what happened. Althaus, on some occasions, discusses the question of the responsibility of man for the fall and then gives a vindication of the spirit of man. Because of the spirit's divine origin, he states that it always tends to what is good and hardly can be thought of as being in opposition to God.[68] (At other occasions he states the response of Adam, pp. 60, 70, 89f.) A consequence of this saying of Althaus must be that the spirit of man cannot be in conscious opposition to God and that the fall consequently must be thought of as something only related to his flesh.

On the other hand, (2) Althaus also talks about the fall as a spiritual event[69] and even observes the role of the free will[70] and maintains the responsibility of Adam. But though he stresses the spiritual aspect, he nevertheless wants to restrict it in what I would consider to be too great a degree. His reasons for this are partly what has already been said, but even the infancy of Adam, which I think he over-emphasizes.[71]

At another time though, I think Althaus speaks quite accurately about Gregory.[72] He here makes the free will of man the basis for his sin, but also wants to bring the changeability of everything created into consideration,[73] which is something we have observed above.[74]

Otis in his article "Cappadocian Thought as a Coherent System" gives full attention to the problems discussed above. His article deals with the Cappadocian theology as a whole, but his ideas will only be discussed here as far as they concern Gregory of Nazianzus.

In introduction we may say that Otis' attitude minimizes and even denies the spiritual aspects of the fall in the understanding of the Cappadocians. This is a matter where he is strongly critical of their theology. He understands them as being unable to offer a full and satisfying account for the sin and fall of man as well as of Satan.

To understand the argumentation of Otis we have to start with his understanding of Origen.[75] When Origen is read, one finds him describing the (prehistoric) fall of the souls and of Satan as an event caused by their free will.[76] At some occasion(s) Origen even tries to explain this fall as caused by satiation or weariness with God.[77] The spiritual beings became satiated with God and thus turned from him. There are here two possibilities of understanding Origen. Either you stress the aspect of freedom as the primary one or the idea of satiation. Otis chooses the second alternative[78] as in his view, the theory of freedom as such does not offer much satisfaction. His reason for this is that according to the Greek idea of fall and sin, none in full knowledge of what he is doing would sin, even if he is free to do that.[79] But the theory of satiation gives an explanation of the fall.

Otis also mentions, as an aspect, the "instability of creatureliness as such".[80] He doesn't make any use of this observation, though it certainly is a category in which we can understand the fall spiritually, even in the Cappadocian theology.

Behind the idea of satiation in the theology of Origen is what Otis calls the Origenistic kind of mysticism and the finitude of the character of God,[81] and his knowability. This idea purports that man is able to reach a full knowledge of God and thus to get tired of him. Thus far is Otis' understanding of Origen.

If we turn to the Cappadocians, Otis now finds another kind of mysticism in their theology. God is no longer totally comprehensible to man,[82] but will be the object of an ever and infinite pursuit. Thus there is no risk that man ever will get tired of him or suffer a fall due to this reason. But this means according to Otis that the Cappadocians cannot make use of the theory of satiation and thus are deprived of this theory as an explanation of the fall and don't have any satisfying explanation of the sin and the fall as a spiritual event.[83]

Now I think Otis is quite right when he observes the difficulties Gregory has concerning the idea of the fall as a spiritual one. Gregory's thinking of the nature of the angels which we have discussed above[84] is probably evidence for this. For Gregory, it seemed to be a problem that the angels could sin. We have seen that probably, due to this reason, he had to attribute to them a certain kind of bodily nature.

Otis further says that the fall of Adam, according to the Cappadocians, only can be attributed to "a) the persuasion of Satan, b) the deception of the fleshly passions, and c) the weakness of the human intellect." He even acknowledges an element of moral culpability, but finds it "very subordinate".[85] Only observing these aspects I think Otis fails to notice the obvious spiritual way in which Gregory actually talks about the fall.

This attitude of Otis is also questioned by G. Ladner in an article in the same volume as the article previously referred to. He there writes, "It seems to me, however, that Professor Otis somewhat overstresses the element of ignorance in the Cappadocians' concept of sin; I cannot quite share his view that this conception accounted for their difficulty in explaining the sin of spiritual creatures, especially of the angels. The Cappadocians' apparent perplexity before the fact that angels and "spiritual" men should choose evil knowingly, seems to me to derive, rather, from a genuine realization of the "mystery of iniquity."[86]

Otis further maintains that sin for the Cappadocians, only belonged to the historic, bodily existence in time (diástema) but was impossible in the eternal, spiritual existence with God.[87] As to whether this actually concerns Gregory must be questioned. When he hints at the greater, more terrible fall that man might have suffered, if he from the beginning had been put in the nearness of God or given the full light, I would understand this as a realization by Gregory of the possibility of a fall in the non-historic, eternal (non-diastemic) existence and life with God. Thus a fall in the spiritual existence with God.

There is yet another remark to be made. On p. 112, Otis discusses the relation of the Cappadocians to Origen and his idea of the prehistoric fall of the souls, for which the bodily life of this creation was meant as a place of correction. When Otis, in the writings of Basil, finds talk of this life as a "schoolhouse and trainingplace"[88] he regards this as very closed to the idea of the prehistoric fall. He states that Basil rejected this idea. When we read St. Gregory we are confronted though with yet another possibility in understanding. Here the material creation is regarded as a training school not because of a previous fall in the world of God but so as to prevent such a thing, which certainly is another idea.

Otis may be right when he stresses the problems of the Cappadocians when they are confronted with the fall. But at any rate, in the writings of Gregory of Nazianzus, we clearly find the fall spoken of as a spiritual event, as we have tried to point out earlier in this chapter.

The attitude of **Portmann** is to stress the aspect of composited-ness though he also observes the spiritual one. He very explicitly notes the idea of Gregory about the freedom of man, his idea of man's free acquiring of the good and further what we have called man's moral "mobility", and even the risk of pride.[89] In spite of this acknowledging of the spiritual aspects, he directly and explicitly states, "The possibility of sin he (Gregory) doesn't base so much upon the freedom of man in contrary to Origen as upon the compositedness of the nature, which is increasing with the greater distance from God".[90]

This statement of Portmann is called into question by **Spidlík**, who stresses the role of the free will for the fall of man.[91] Spidlík accordingly puts the main accent on the spiritual aspect though he even discusses the weakness of man, which we have pointed out earlier, and the risk which is related to his composite nature.

Plagnieux stresses the spiritual aspect and the freedom of man.[92] He emphasizes the immaturity of Adam, his weakness, and the character of the fall as an early eating of the forbidden tree. He regards the fall as an negligence rather than a direct insurrection against God.

Winslow, at last, does not regard the fall as due to the flesh of man, "rather man's original disobedience was spiritual and noetic, free and rational."[93]

6.m. Two aspects of the fall:
a) as a spiritual event, b) as related to composition

In the thinking of Gregory there are a number of somewhat different aspects to the fall. We have, on the one hand, understood it as a spiritual and personal event of man as a free being, and on the other hand, we have found a relating of sin to the composited-ness of man.

How are these two aspects to be related to each other, and is it actually possible to relate them to each other? The different emphasis of the authors referred to above bears witness to the difficulties I think we find here. To begin with, I think we are right to state that the spiritual, personal aspect is the dominant one. But what about the idea of the composite nature of man as a cause for his tendency to sin? If Gregory understood the fall to have been caused by man as a free being, why then was it necessary to relate it to his doubleness? It does not seem quite logical. Otis is thus probably quite right when he observes the problem of the Cappadocians concerning the fall as a spiritual event. Gregory's sayings about the fall of Lucifer and the nature of the angels testify to that. But I think it goes much too far to draw the conclusion that Gregory thus was unable to think of the fall in spiritual terms.

We may understand Gregory as recognizing a kind of instability in everything created (which I understand as a moral instability). Perhaps also, he may regard this instability in terms of composition and a lack of total simplicity.

7. The reasons for the composite nature of man

In the preceding sections, we have discussed Gregory's understanding of the primordial state of man, his original immaturity, the fall of man and his original tendency toward sin and transgression of God's command. We are now able to return to the main theme of this chapter, Gregory's reflections and ideas about the reasons for the composite nature of man and his bodily character.

In the beginning of the chapter some texts were presented wherein Gregory deals with this issue. Reading these texts we found quite a number of ideas and reflections among which we were able to discern three main aspects or leading ideas. We will now continue with the discussion of these aspects.

7.a. The tendency to sin and fall

In several of the texts Gregory relates the bodily nature of man to his tendency to sin and fall. We will start the discussion at this point. In the preceding paragraphs the fall of man has been thoroughly discussed, and we found quite a variety of things which have to be taken into consideration.

We even found that we have to distinguish between the actual fall of Adam and the greater fall, which should be avoided, and from which man should be protected. When Gregory is looking for the significance of the body, he now relates it to both kinds of falls. We will begin by examining the latter.

a) Avoidance of the "greater" fall

What we are confronted with here is the very specific and exceptional idea of Gregory which we have earlier described and discussed. The idea that man should be protected from the great and terrible kind of fall that Lucifer suffered, the fall of a spiritual being put in the nearness of God and previously given the full light of God. How could this be avoided? Reading the texts where this idea of Gregory is expressed it is evident that he here found a kind of protective function of the body.

The "bodily darkness" has been placed like a "cloud" between us and God.[94] As a mixed being, man is put at a distance from God and thus protected from an overly risky nearness to him.[95]

We here even have to take the idea of the infancy of Adam into consideration. Gregory never explicitly relates this to the avoiding of the "greater" fall, but there is evidently a type of interrelationship between these ideas in his theology. Adam, for Gregory, was a human being who, in the beginning, only to a certain degree partook of the divine light. The fuller participation of the divine light and the fuller knowledge of God was still in his future. When we contrast this with the idea of the protection from the "greater" fall, this must be regarded as an aspect of the infancy of Adam.

In this passage however our attention concerns the function of the body. For Gregory, the matter as such was the kind of nature that was at a distance from God.[96] Thanks to his participation in material nature, through his body and during his earthly life, man is placed at the same distance from God and protected from a nearness to him that may prove to be too riskful.[97]

Over against this idea of Gregory, may a question now be logically formulated. What will happen when man finally reaches the life with God and the risky nearness to him? Once in heaven, is there any guarantee that he will not then suffer a disastrous fall after all? There is even a kind of answer to this question in the thinking of Gregory, more or less directly expressed. We will discuss this further in section 7.b., but, in anticipation, I think we are right to say that it is precisely at this point, as an answer to this question, that Gregory searches out one of his reasons for the bodily nature of man and hence his earthly life. In attempting to formulate it, we may say that the earthly life has got a kind of strengthening significance for the character of man, whether he is fallen or not. During the life on earth, in waiting and longing for the life with God and "wrestling with that here below",[98] the character of man might be strengthened and so the risk for a fall in the heavenly life eliminated.

I have called this idea of Gregory a very specific one. As far as I know he is the only among the Fathers who expresses it, and that is worth noticing. The relation to Origen in this respect has been discussed above.[99] It is likely that the theology of Origen, with his idea of the prehistoric fall in the pure spiritual world, has influenced Gregory's thinking in this respect. We may say that Origen drew Gregory's attention to the possibility and risk of a fall even in the heavenly sphere and life. Gregory's own idea may be regarded as an answer to Origen as well as an alternative, which still pays attention to the kind of risk of lapse to which we may say the theology of Origen drew the attention. At this point Gregory seems to agree with Origen.

In actual fact, there are very few texts where we find this idea of the fall that should be avoided.[100] But we have to acknowledge its interrelationship to and connection with the rest of the theology of Gregory. It is a logical and fully consistent part of the system of Gregory as we now attempt to reconstruct it. It should certainly be noticed and observed.

b) The body as a "paidagogia" and chastiment for the fallen man

Gregory does however even look for the significance of the body as related to the sinfulness of man and the tendency to fall in another way. We may express his idea like this. In creating man, God is foreseeing the possibility of the transgression and the fall, and because of that gives man a body as a means of correction and chastiment. It has the function of a "paidagogia"[101] of the fallen man. In Or. 38.10 we find this idea. Man was "at the same time spirit and flesh, spirit because of the grace, flesh because of the pride. The one that he might continue to live and give honour to his benefactor. The other that he might suffer and in suffering be reminded and corrected if he became proud of his greatness."

In a similar way, the same idea is expressed in Or. 14.7 (above). In this oration, for which the theme is the love of the poor, Gregory talks with compassion about the opressed and the sick and that causes him to go into an extended exposition on the body. In a form of dialectic, he both blames the body and praises it, as an enemy and a cooperator and asks for the significance of the troubles it causes.

When we look at these two texts (Or. 14.6—7 and 38.10) and Gregory's attitude to the body, we find two closely related aspects.

1) One of them looks more to the lowliness of the body and its low nature. Perhaps we may express this idea of Gregory like this. Man may, because of his greatness as a divine being, be seized by vain hybris and overevaluate himself (which of course effects his relation to God, his maker). But if and when that happens he has a kind of corrective reminder in the lowliness of the body. Its lowliness may help him to a proper understanding and evaluation of himself.

2) The second aspect more looks to the troubles of the body and the suffering it originates. If man exalts himself and becomes "proud of his greatness", "despising his Creator", the troubles of the body cause him to look to God and the sufferings become a kind of recalling to God. The sufferings are a kind of correction to his pride, and the tendency of man to despise God is corrected by man's need of him in his trouble.

Thus is Gregory able to find a benefit in the troublesome bodily life. In doing this, there might be a tendency to glorify trouble and suffering, but this is hardly the case in the texts referred to. Or. 14 is a testimony to the contrary. Here Gregory expresses his compassion toward the oppressed and sick and his comments on the body are very rash. He talks about "this troublesome and low and faithless body" and calls it an enemy and fetter.

But even in the same sentence, the body is talked about as fellow servant and cooperator and a "fellow servant I love". In this I think we find a good expression of the double attitude of Gregory to the body. It is both friend and enemy. Gregory is perhaps also thinking of the passions of the body and therein lies danger for man.

I think we may say that the starting point for Gregory is the bad experience of the body and of man's earthly life. And in regard to both this and wrestling with the problems of theodicy, he looks for some sense and meaning to oppression and suffering. One of his responses to this dilemma is the idea which we discuss in this section. Perhaps God, when he created man, foresaw the fall and the sinfulness and the errors of man and therefore created him as a blended being because of the "paidagogia" that the bodily life would make possible and offer.[102]

7.b. Man may himself acquire "the good" and the life with God

What we will now discuss are some of the more interesting ideas in the theology of Gregory. In some of the texts referred to in this chapter,[103] Gregory expresses the idea that the reason for the bodily life of man might be so that he himself may inherit and gain "the good" and the life with God, and not only receive this as a gift. Hence, Gregory finds a reason for the troublesome life on earth and for "the struggle and wrestling with that here below".[104] Free to choose "the good" himself, (thanks to his free will), man shall make it his own, "not only sown in his nature"[105] but also acquire it for himself. After struggling with "that here below", he may get the object of his hope as a prize of virtue and not only as the gift of God.[106]

Though Gregory only at some occasions and rather briefly mentions these ideas, his formulations are full of interesting aspects. As noted earlier, this seems to be a special capacity of his, the ability to formulate suggestive and interesting ideas with rather few words.

The different aspects of these texts, to a certain extent, have been discussed by Althaus and Portmann though with a slightly different accent. Precisely due to the brevity of these formulations, I think they are open to different interpretations, and I even think this openness is a part of their value. In this context I think we must be careful not to overinterpret them, but even in trying to avoid this temptation, I think we are still able to discern three different aspects or poles in the formulations of Gregory. It may even be regarded as a confirmation of this observation that each of these three aspects is found in the interpretations by Althaus and Portmann of Gregory, though they do not explicitly discuss different aspects or formulate them themselves in this manner. The three different aspects are: a) a more "meritorious" and "virtuous" one, b) a more "personal" one, and finally c) a corrective one, which may be said to concern a strengthening of the character of man. These aspects all belong together, and perhaps we would do better to speak of different accents. I think we need this systematizing though as a help for discussion and understanding of Gregory.

The general, common idea, to which both Althaus and Portmann draw our attention, is that man, only by the action of the free will, is able to practise virtue and acquire what is good.[107] Only that which is based on a decision of the free will is virtue. Thus the freedom of man is of basic significance for his virtue and for his eventual reaching of what Althaus labels "moral perfection".[108]

Portmann here has shown the relationship of Gregory's thought to the common Greek understanding of virtue. "In der Freiheit wurzeln den Griechen die sittlichen Werte. Für Sokrates-Platon ist Tugend gleich Wissen, ein echtes Wissen allerdings, das die Tat in sich trägt und gebiert. Zufällig, 'unbewusst' etwas Gutes tun heisst nichts. Das Tun verstehend beherrschen und zu seinem erkannten Ziele führen, heisst wirklich frei handeln und das getane Gute als eigenes besitzen. Dieser altgriechische Freiheitsbegriff wirkt auch bei Gregor von Nazianz nach." [109]

With this as a background, it is easier to understand the ideas of Gregory and his reflections that man is perhaps to receive what he is longing for as a "prize of virtue".[110] Thus we may observe the virtuous and meritorious aspect (a).

There is though even a personal one (b) involved in the ideas just described. The good is something that man himself is able to acquire and make his own. We find this very clearly expressed in Or. 38.12, where Gregory says that God honoured man with the gift of free will "in order that the good may belong to the choosing one no less than to him who produced the seeds [of it]". Thus the earthly and bodily life of man might be regarded as the place where man himself makes the good his own as a free being, and the personal aspect of this may be noticed.

Althaus also gives attention to this personal aspect (without using this term). He observes the fact that in this text, Or. 38.12, man is said to be the owner of the good just as it belongs to God himself and adds, "Man should thus in creation have the rank of a partner granted equality of rights".[111] Finally we shall turn to the last aspect (c) which we found in the formulations of Gregory. This concerns what we may call a strengthening of man's character. In Or. 28.12, we met the idea that if man did not have to work hard, he might risk letting go again of what he had acquired. We have even met a kind of testing and purifying aspect in some of the texts (Or. 2.17 and 28.12). We have earlier discussed the fact that the first man, according to Gregory, was afflicted by a kind of moral weakness. Relating this to the "strenghtening" and "purifying" aspect we may understand him to mean that the bodily life may purify man from his weakness and strengthen his character. The risk that man should move in the direction of evil might in this way be overcome. We have met the stress on free choice, so that by this choice man may make the good his own and hold fast to it. Portmann observes this and states that only that which emanates from a free decision "will gain persistence".[112] In an earlier section[113] we discussed the risk of a great fall and ended with a crucial question. What about man when he once will reach his heavenly goal and life? Does anything guarantee that he will not then after all suffer the great and disastrous fall of becoming proud of his status as the image of God? Perhaps we here find a kind of answer to this question.

Gregory evidently realized the risk involved in the spiritual life of man with God and we have supposed Origen to be the inspirer of that thinking.[114] (I think we have to realize that this risk for them was a real one and not only a logical or intellectual possibility). Now we are perhaps here discernng Gregory's own answer to that problem. Through the earthly and bodily life, the dangerous tendency to sin might be overcome, and man's character strengthened. In that way, once reaching heaven and the life with God, he will hold fast to it and preserve the good he has acquired by himself. All this is according to the principle that man values higher that which he has had to long for and struggle to obtain.

One of the aspects of bodily life on earth then is that the dangerous risk of a greater fall might be overcome. It is this that we may call the answer of Gregory to Origen, if the latter is to be understood as counting on repeated falls, and the specific alternative of Gregory.

A particular understanding of the existence of man as a possible consequence of the thinking of St. Gregory

I want to stress the existential implications of what has just been discussed. As already stated, this certainly was not only of a theoretical or logical interest to Gregory, but a part of his understanding of the problem of evil and sin. We may even say that his formulations point to a certain understanding of man and his existence.

I will therefore finally complete this section by bringing the discussion even one step further and show some consequences which might be drawn from the theology of Gregory. It should clearly and explicitly be said that Gregory himself never draws these conclusions explicitly or discusses them. They may rather be said to be an inherent possibility in this theology, or a possibility of an anthropological understanding, with the thinking of Gregory as a base.

When Gregory is describing the first primordial man we found him looking upon man as morally movable into two directions. We further said that his way of speaking gives the impression of somebody who is standing before two possibilities.[115] Going one step further, and interpreting Gregory's thought, even before the fall, this primordial man may be understood as someone with a choice placed before him who has not yet made up his mind. This may be understood as related to the existence of man as such, our own, as well as the "first" man's. It can be taken as a description of life as such.

To be created is to have to make a choice. As long as man has not decided he is wavering[116] in two directions, with a possibility to move in either of them. In order to hold to the good and even to become good, he has to decide this himself through choosing by his free will. And as long as he has not, the risk remains. Accordingly, this risk even must be included in the primordial—"newly created"—situation of man (even before the fall) and remain until he has taken his decision. In reading and interpreting Gregory, we may understand the earthly life as the place where that can happen and as the place for the inevitable decision that belongs to personal existence as such.

Following Gregory, we may understand this as a way to exclude and overcome the dangerous risk of the greater fall. But this might even be understood in a more personal way. We may understand the earthly life as life at a distance from God, where man is given the possibility himself to choose God and thus by a personal act come into contact with him.

7.c. A microcosm motif

In conclusion, we shall direct our attention to the last of the three main aspects we have found in the texts. We may here talk about a kind of microcosm motif in the thinking of Gregory though he himself generally does not use this term for man as a mixed being.[117] This line of thought is not as dominant as the others in the texts and is even a rather different one.

We here come upon the ancient, non-Christian as well as Christian idea of man as a sort of microcosm or little world. This, in short, refers to an understanding of an analogy between man and the greater cosmos.[118] Man, as Gregory talks about him, sums up the two different kinds of natures in himself, the spiritual and the material. He is further talked about as having a kind of middle position between God and the material world. (In Or. 2.17 this middle position concerns the soul in relation to God and the body.) We may understand this middle position to be related to and caused by man's mixed nature.

What we shall now observe is the status of man and his role and function. We may understand this as a consequence of his middle position as a mixed being. Man is thus a king on earth as well as a praiser of God.

In comparison to the other ideas discussed in this chapter we may here even notice a shift of interest. We have, in the discussions of the two other main aspects, found reflections which all concern the benefit for man of the body and, we may say, of the earthly life. Now, on the contrary, Gregory talks of a function of man; the soul has got a task vis-a-vis the body.[119] That is to bring it to God (a faint suggestion of man as a kind of mediator as concerning matter and its relation to God), and we may further say that the mixing of man is for the sake of God who is now praised even on the earth.[120]

Chapter 4

The theological system of Gregory. Some characteristic structures of it

1. Introduction

Reading the texts of Gregory it is possible to observe that man as a double and mixed being forms and constitutes a part of what might be called a theological system, and that this system further is characterized by certian structures or patterns.

In this chapter this theological "system" shall be dealt with as well as the structures or features which I think characterize it. Gregory himself does not talk about his thinking as a kind of "system", but the passages in Or. 38.7—13, as well as the dogmatic poems have more or less such a character. Thus, reading the texts we are able to discern something which might be called a theological system, though not equally completely worked out in all its "parts".

What I mean with a "system" here is the ontological or metaphysical side or aspect of the theology of Gregory, consisting of his understanding of creation, man, incarnation and the final theosis and goal in the life with God, whereas the aspects of his thinking concerning salvation and the history of salvation are left aside.

If we now in this manner look upon the theology of Gregory step by step, a system becomes discernable which further has a certain characteristic construction and certain characteristic patterns.

In the first part of this chapter, the theological system of Gregory will be dealt with as it is possible to understand it from the texts referred to above and to reconstruct it from these texts and the rest of the writings of Gregory.

In the second part the structures or patterns referred to above will be discussed. It should be stated here that these structures in general are discernable rather to the readers of the texts than stressed by Gregory himself.

Discussing these structures I at last think it is possible to discern and observe that Gregory, who in high a degree was a Platonizing thinker, both belongs to this tradition as well as differs and diverges from it.

2. Creation

When we look upon the theology of Gregory from the point of view of it constituting a system, we are first confronted with the existence of God, the one who really is.[1]

But as God, being goodness, wanted "that the objects of his kindness might be more" he let the created worlds come into existence. Generally Gregory does not say much about the reasons of God for creation,[2] but in Or. 38.9 he as quoted above looks for motivation in the goodness of God.[3]

In another text, PD 4.63f Gregory motivates the creation in a somewhat different way:

"The Highest ruling over empty aeons moved Himself seeing His beauty's kindly light, the same light of equal excellence of the Deity, shining in a threefold light as it is manifest only for the Deity and those belonging to God. And He moved Himself seeing the types of the world which He had made in His great thoughts, the world creating Mind, [the world] that should become thereafter but even was present for God." Here Gregory makes a reference to what might be called an inner life of God and a contemplating of God himself of his threefold light.[4] And in this Gregory now is seeing the first step of creation. Althaus here observes how Gregory tries to relate the inner-Trinitarian life of God and his outward activity, and further notices that this is done with the use of the Platonic ideas.[5]

So God gives existence to the creation. Turning to the way in which Gregory talks about the event of creation we shall start with observing two things. The first (1) concerns the character of creation as a *giving existence to*, and the other (2) concerns what I want to call *the two-step character* of creation and of the creative activity or event.

3. Creation as giving existence to

When Gregory talks about the creation and the creative activity of God he does not make use of one special term for this activity but uses a variety of differentiated terms. In Or. 38.9, to give an example, he says that God, or rather the Good, when he wanted to multiply the objects for his goodness "conceived the angelic and heavenly powers. And this conception was a work fulfilled by the Word and perfected by the Spirit. And so the secondary splendours came into being (ὑπέστησαν)". As in this passage along with words designating a making or a creating act[6] Gregory is using terms with the meaning of giving existence to and become. Thus a term used is "ὑφιστάναι"[7] with the meaning "cause to exist, make".

In the same way in some texts Gregory uses the word "γίγνεσθαι"[8] to become, come into being. In Or. 45.28 he thus states, "We came into being that we may receive benefits", and in another passage, Or. 32.7, Gregory, with a similar vocabulary, talks about the one who "gave existence (τὸ εἶναι) to that which did not exist (τὰ οὐκ ὄντα).[9]

Of these terms I now think the latter ones with the meaning of giving existence to and becoming should be understood as the more specifically qualified ones.

For Gregory, God is the one who always is,[10] without a beginning,[11] and in some texts we find him contrasting God and man.[12] In Or. 42.17 we find Gregory distinguishing God and the creation (κτίσμα) and arguing against the idea that any of the divine Persons in the Trinity should be a creation. "If [he is] God, [he is] not a creation. For the creation ranks with us who are not gods. But if [he is] a creation [he is] not God, for it began in time. And there was [a time] when that which had a beginning, was not. That for which non existence (τὸ οὐκ εἶναι) was prior, is not that which exists in the proper sense (κυρίως). But that which in the proper sense has not being, how is that God?"[13]

Thus we find Gregory talking and thinking of the created things and beings as something that has become, and has come into existence. I think we are right to look for a background to this in the common Greek thinking for which matter was eternal, and thus coeternal to the divine nature or Being. We now find Gregory talking in contrast to this about creation as something that has become and now has existence. In one text, "the poem of the world", Gregory even consciously creates a polemic against the Greek idea of the eternal nature of the world. Matter and form were not with God from the beginning (sunarchós).[14]

4. The two-step character of creation

When we look upon the way in which Gregory is talking about the creation and the creative activity of God, we find a kind of differentiation of this action or event which, systematically speaking, may be called a 2-step structure or pattern. (In Or. 38.9 there is even a third "step" or moment which will be discussed in the next chapter.)[15]

Thus we find Gregory talking about both (1) the conceiving or initiating of God of the world, and (2) the actual performance and fulfilling of this idea. In Or. 38.9 for instance, Gregory talks about God conceiving the angelic powers, "a work fulfilled by the Word and perfected by the Spirit."

This two-step pattern is especially notable in the poem on the creation of the world. Here Gregory describes how God first conceives the world and how the forms or ideas take on existence in his thoughts, and how the "worldcreating Mind" thereafter brings forth the world.[16]

So the first "step" of the event of creation is the conception of it in the thoughts of God. The same two-step pattern is even found in some other texts.

In *PD* 8.55—56, Gregory talks about Logos who created the world "following the design of the great Father".[17]

We may thus talk about a first "step" of the creating act as a conceiving or initiating of the creation, and about the actual performance of it as a second "step".

Further commenting on this, we may say that this kind of description puts emphasis on the origin of the creation as being within God himself. This is also effected by the kind of "emanative" vocabulary which Gregory sometimes is using and which shall be discussed further on.[18]

5. The creation of the two worlds

Gregory's way of presenting the actual creating by God of the creation has already received attention and been discussed in chapter 2 and shall not be repeated here in detail. We found then that Gregory first described the creation of the two worlds, the spiritual or noetic one and the material one.[19] Of these two worlds the spiritual or angelic one is understood as being near God, though Gregory even knows about a kind of distance between God and this angelic world as expressed in some texts.[20] The other one, the material world, on the other hand is understood as being at a distance from God.[21] It should be remarked that Gregory also knows about a nearness of God to the world, even the material one as noticed earlier.[22] When we look upon the "system" of Gregory, it is the "distance" rather than the nearness that constitutes the characteristic features of it.

We are here confronted with a distance between the two created worlds as well with a distance between God and the material one. As previously mentioned, Gregory even knows about a kind of distance between the angels and God, and on the whole we from some texts may talk about a distance between God and creation as such, that is, between God and everything created. In Or. 6.22, Gregory can state that the Trinity "let the whole creation be outside [itself], the one creation kept off by the first veil, the other by the second. By the first veil is meant the heavenly and angelic creation kept off from the Deity, by the second is ours kept off from the heavenly [natures]."[23]

6. Man as a mingling of the two kinds of created natures

We next find Gregory talking about the creation of man as mingling of the two different kinds of natures, the material and the spiritual. This aspect of man and his twofold nature has already been discussed. From the thinking of Gregory about man as being a single being, (though a composite being) we may talk about a uniting of the two contrasted natures in man even though we have seen that the unity or one-ness of man in his earthly condition or state, might be said to be relative to a certain degree.[24] We have also in the preceding chapter discussed the implications for man, in different aspects, of the mixed and composed nature. Now we shall observe some different aspects related to man as a mixed being.

1. In man, two different and contrasted natures, the material and the spiritual, are mixed and united. As previously pointed out,[25] it should be observed that whereas the material component of man is taken from the already existing earth, his spiritual nature, the soul, is a new creation "inbreathed" at the moment of creation and thus not taken from the already existing spiritual creation. When Gregory stresses the creation of man as a mixture, and a bringing together of the two different natures, this should not be taken too literally. In Or. 38.11 we do find Gregory consciously talking about the two kinds of natures or qualities, "mind" and "sense" as separate from each other though. There was not yet any mingling of the two opposite natures. The creation of man is further talked about as a mingling of them, and we have further regarded this as a kind of representative mingling, mirroring the two parts or spheres of the world,[26] rather than a union of them literally speaking.

So we find in man a mingling of spiritual and material creation. The divine character of man has earlier been noticed and the "strong" language Gregory sometimes is using, has been observed.[27] Man is "a part of God".[28] If we now even take this aspect of man in consideration we may regard his doubleness as a bringing together of something material and something divine or yet even more strongly speak of a communication between God and something material.[29] Man, thanks to his soul, may be regarded as a kind of representative of the spiritual and divine sphere.

2. By the soul, the body of man is brought to God in the final goal of man. The "distance" between God and the material creation is mentioned above. Through man, in the form of the body, we now, systematically speaking, see this distance bridged over to some extent and lessened, (though Gregory himself not is talking in terms of diminishing a distance here).

We have earlier noted, on the basis of some texts, that Gregory seems to reckon with a change of the bodily character in the heavenly existence.[30] If we are correct here (in talking about a spiritualized body and even about a divine character to it), we now may talk about the body as being less different in its character, both from the spirit or soul of man and from God himself. Thus happens a diminishing of the differences and contrast in that which concerns quality and character.

We have at last, even a possible way of understanding Gregory as he talked about the body and soul of man as being united together higher and more closely in the future state of man.[31]

Summarizing, we now find systematically speaking, through man in the theology of Gregory, a bringing together of different and separate natures in two respects. a) Spiritual and material creation, and b) God and matter in the form of the body of man.

We have earlier understood this bringing of the body to God as related to man's final theosis. From the texts where this task of man is talked about[32] this bringing of the body to God by the soul could be understood as something that man is achieving himself and by himself. It is clear though that Gregory understood this as related to the task of Christ and the incarnation of God[33] just as on the whole he regarded the "divine-making" of man as something brought about by Christ (as well as by the Spirit).[34] This now leads us to the next "step" in the thinking of Gregory in regard to a "system", the incarnation and the union of God and man in Christ.

7. Christ, the new mingling

In the writings of Gregory we find Christ being talked about as "a new mingling",[35] a mixing of God and man. The task here is not to give a full account and a thorough discussion of the Christology[36] of Gregory and his work in that respect. What shall here be discussed is his understanding of Christ from the point of view of this chapter, specifically the attempt to regard the thinking of Gregory as a theological system. We shall look upon the function of Christ and the incarnation from this point of view and further bring into consideration what is essential for the later discussion of the structures and characteristics of this "system".

In introduction it should be stated that it was Gregory's interest to vindicate the *full divinity* of Christ as well as his *full human nature*. Christ was fully God.[37] On the other hand, in regard to the human aspect of Christ, in the Christological controversy Gregory asserted the fullness and completeness of his human nature. God was united or mingled not only with flesh, but even with a human soul and mind.[38]

Another characteristic of his Christology is the stressing of the unity or *oneness* of Christ. There are not "two sons".[39] With certain specific formulations Christ is said to be "one and the same",[40] or "one out of two", or "out of both".[41]

We shall so begin the discussion with the *parallel* which we find between the Christology of Gregory and his anthropology. This parallel is especially striking because of the vocabulary Gregory uses. Talking, on the one hand, about man and on the other about Christ, Gregory in certain respects makes use of the same or similar kinds of expressions and terms.

We have seen that for the compounded nature of man Gregory uses terms with the meaning of *mixture* and *mingling*.[42] Talking about the union and uniting in Christ of divine and human nature he now is using the same or similar terms.[43] The incarnation or the assumption of flesh of God is called the "new mingling". We may illustrate this with Or. 2.23 where this is expressed as "... the assumed flesh, ... the new mingling, God and man, one of both and both through one". Christ is here not only called a mixture, but the new one.[44] Like this Gregory is stressing the parallel between Christ and what happens in man. In both cases we find two different kinds of elements or natures brought together and "mixed".

Even for the union or one-ness of the different elements the same or similar vocabulary is used. In Or. 38.11, which deals with the double nature of man as a compound, he is said to be "one living being of both" the visible and invisible nature, an expression similar to the one which we have found used for Christ.[45]

8. Created and uncreated nature

In Or. 38.13 Gregory talks about "the strange blending" when "the one who is (ὁ ὤν) becomes and the uncreated is created".[46] In this way in some texts Gregory emphasizes the double aspect of Christ, that of being both God and created. He is the invisible one who becomes visible, the one above time who "begins",[47] the one who at the same time is heavenly and earthly.[48] In antithetical language, to which Portmann draws our attention,[49] Gregory talks like this about Christ, ascribing to him the properties of God as well of the creation.

In man we have met a mixing of two contrasted elements, material and spiritual, and we have observed the manner in which Gregory talks about these two components of man as different and contrasted.[50] In the Christology, systematically speaking, we are now confronted with a mingling of two other elements or components, namely uncreated and created nature. The parallel between the anthropology and the Christology has already been mentioned. This parallel is even noticeable in the dialectical language with which Gregory talks about the components in the two "blendings". So he talks about man as "earthly and heavenly, temporal and immortal, visible and intellectual ... at the same time spirit and flesh",[51] and on one occasion in a similar way he talks about Christ; "... at the same time earthly and heavenly, visible and intellectual, comprehensible and incomprehensible".[52] It should be observed though that the blending in the one case is a mixing of two created elements, and in the other of created and uncreated nature.

9. The mediatory function of soul or mind in Christ

One of the interests of Gregory was, as previously mentioned, to vindicate the full human character of Christ. In him all the "parts" of man were found, body and soul as well as mind. What should be here observed is the special function of the soul or mind in Christ as Gregory understood it.

For Gregory, as for all Platonizing thinking, the divine or the highest reality and the material natures were two contrasted natures or spheres. The idea of bringing them together and uniting them must thus for this kind of thinking be a paradoxical one and I even think we are right to say in clear contrast to the basic understanding of God and matter as being at a kind of distance from each other. (This is a distance which we do not find bridged over in the different Platonic systems or sketches of systems, but rather "filled out" by certain intermediary Beings or spheres.)[53]

This basic idea of the divine and material spheres as being separate is also Gregory's as we have seen. Yet in Christ they are brought together according to Gregory's understanding of him. And here the soul in Christ has a special function. In some texts we find Gregory talking particularly about soul or mind as having a kind of "middle" position and "mediatory" function in Christ. In Or. 2.23, as quoted before, Gregory talks about "the new mingling" of God and man, and says that "God was mixed with flesh by a soul between (ψυχὴ μεσή) and the separate (alt. different) [natures] were bound together by the kinship (οἰκειότης) to each of the mediating one". In Or. 38.13, Gregory talks in a similar way about the "rational soul" in Christ, "mediating between the deity and the thickness of the flesh" and in Ep. 101, col. 188 the same is said about "mind".

The rational soul, or in some texts the "mind", is thus understood as having a kind of middle position between the divine and the fleshly. It is a "mediating" factor between the deity and the flesh. I think we are right to regard this expression and this understanding of the role of the soul as a proof of the understanding of God and matter in opposition to one another to which we previously referred. In the text quoted,[54] this function of the soul is even talked about as related to a certain kinship or affinity (οἰκειότης) to both the opposite natures (God and flesh) in Christ.

In these texts, Gregory talks about the soul as well as the mind. We have earlier found that Gregory generally uses a bipartite partition of man, which means that the soul is understood as the spiritual or rational element in man in contrast to the body or the fleshly component. Sometimes he though is using a tripartite (and even fourpartite) "division" and talks about body, soul and mind.[55] Through different vocabulary used in the texts discussed in this paragraph we find a proof of this alternating use of a bipartite and a tripartite division of man respectively. The idea is though the same, in Christ the rational or spiritual "part" of his human nature has a middle position between God and flesh and a mediating role and function.

10. Not only an anthropological but a universal significance of the incarnation?

The relation of Christ to the divinisation of man has previously been taken into consideration. In this section the question shall be put as to whether Gregory saw an even wider cosmological or universal significance in the coming of Christ and the union of created and uncreated in him. This not only concerns man but the creation as such and as a whole.

In some texts we now find evidence that Gregory was thinking in such a direction. In Or. 7.24 he talks about God not only as the Maker but even as the "Transformer of all by the artisan Word", and in Or. 21.25, the second coming of Christ is mentioned together with and in relation to a "renovation" and a "trans-reformation" (μεταποίησις) and change (μετάθεσις) of all.[56]

In these texts this transformation is simply mentioned without any longer exposition of the theme. In one text though, the *fourth theological oration*, Or. 30 we find a theologically more extensive exposition. Here the reformation (metapoiēsis) is related to the "time of restitution"[57] when all will be subjected to Christ, the Son, and the Son will subject all to the Father.[58] And when further "God shall be all in all" and "Christ all and in all".[59]

In this text, which is a central one in the material as it belongs to the theological orations, we find the idea expressed that the "time of restitution" will implicate a bringing of all to God and what must be understood as a kind of bringing together of God and creation, God shall be all in all. This kind of thinking is never expressed in any other text. From the systematic point of view, this though is an important idea. As a basic element in the thinking of Gregory we have met the idea of a distance of God to the material creation and even to everything created. In Christ we have found a blending and a bringing together of God and created nature, and now in this text we find what may be systematically labelled an "extending" of this bringing together of God and created nature to "all" by the mission of Christ. This is a bringing of all to God which must be understood to imply a bridging over of the basic distance just referred to (though perhaps with the restriction made earlier.[60])

A typical characteristic of the thinking of Gregory is the idea of a bringing together of different natures such as we have met in man and in Christ. The idea of a final "bringing together" of God and all creation would be consequential to this, and perhaps we should expect a further development of the ideas found in the fourth theological oration in the rest of the writings of Gregory. This though is not the case.[61] Compared with other elements and ideas in the thinking of Gregory this is a less developed one, though certainly a coherent and logical one in the theology of Gregory when regarded as a whole and as a system.

11. Some characteristic structures or patterns in the system of Gregory

In the first part of this chapter we have gone through the theological system of Gregory and its different "parts" or elements. We have discussed the giving of existence by God to creation, the bringing together of its two kinds of natures in man, and the further bringing together of God and created nature in Christ, the new blending. We have observed the task of man to bring the body to God in his final goal, the divinisation by Christ and the Spirit. Finally, we have noticed the idea which is hinted at of a bringing of "all" to God by Christ, and the end of all as the event or condition when God shall be all in all.

In this later part of the chapter we shall go on with a discussion of some characteristics of the "system" of Gregory as it has been understood here. Particular things to be observed are some structures or patterns by which I propose we are able to discern and characterize the system as a whole. Three such structures or patterns which are of a fundamental character in the theology and the thinking of Gregory shall be discussed.

1) The first of them concerns an understanding of a *hierarchy of natures* or different levels of being and reality (divine, spiritual, material). This hierarchical structure is of a basic nature in the thinking of Gregory as it will later be discussed, and belongs to the presuppositions for much of his thinking and also to a certain degree for the other two "structures" that will be discussed here.

2) Next, what might be called the *dialectical character* of the system of Gregory shall be considered. What is here aimed for is a dominant feature in the thinking of Gregory which concerns, (a) an idea of different elements and natures talked about as contrasted and even understood as separate and at a distance from each other, and (b) an idea of a bringing together of the same elements.

3) Finally, we will observe a third characteristic of the thinking of Gregory. This is a pattern of *a direction or a movement away from God and a direction or movement "back" to God*. This pattern is especially noticeable and possible to discern in Gregory's idea of man, but also even to some degree in his understanding of creation as such and its relationship to God.

12. A Hierarchy of natures

A typical feature of Platonic thinking is the idea of a hierarchic structure of the existing reality as composed of different levels of beings or realities beginning with a highest sphere or Being and "going down" to the lowest one, the material one or matter (hýle) as such. The different parts or levels of this hiearchy are not identically understood in the different systems or sketches of systems which are found within this tradition and for which no account shall be given or discussion carried on here. Common to them all though are the ideas of a highest level or reality, a rational or/and divine one, and at the bottom of the hierarchy the material level and matter as such. These two levels are understood as being at a kind of distance from each other, and this must be said to be one of the fundamental features of this kind of thinking, never questioned within this tradition itself and of a type of axiomatic nature.[62]

A further characteristic is the idea of one or several intermediary Beings or levels between the highest and the lowest levels. So in the system of Plotin for instance, between the highest Being, "the One", and matter, we find the levels of Mind and of the higher and lower Soul and the individual souls.

As a point of introduction it should be stated in concern to Gregory, that he must, on the one hand, be said to belong to this tradition, but that his thinking, on the other hand, in certain important and striking respects differs from this tradition and perhaps even must be said to break with it and contradict some of its basic assumptions.

In the basic structuring of reality Gregory clearly belongs to the tradition to which has just been referred. Regarding his system we thus are able to discern a tripartite (and even fourpartite) "division" and talks about body, soul and nature), the spiritual, and lastly, the material. Of these three the middle one, the spiritual, has got a kind of middle position, and we may observe this middle position in the anthropology and the Christology as well as the mediatory function of this middle level with regard to the two others.[63]

In the thinking of Gregory, this three level structure must be said to be of a basic and fundamental importance. It belongs to the presuppositions for Gregory's understanding of man and of the incarnation. And it further partly constitutes the basis for the two other patterns or structures that will be discussed here.

Thus far are we able to understand Gregory within the ancient Platonic tradition. But, in a certain respect and at a certain "point" in his system, he breaks this hierarchical pattern in his theology, and that must at least be observed here though it leads us beyond the theme of this study. What I am aiming at is Gregory's *understanding of God* and the three divine hypostases. With the kind of theology which Gregory develops as the proper understanding of God and the three divine Hypostases, the whole idea of a hierarchy which even includes the upper divine sphere with its different Beings must be understood as broken. For Gregory, the three divine Hypostases, the Father, the Son or the Mind of God and the Spirit, were understood as being on the same level and identical in what concerns their nature and divinity. Thus, they do not form a hierarchy with different levels. The interest of Gregory in this respect was to vindicate the sameness of the divinity and to deny all ideas of the Son and the Spirit as being of a less rank and of different and lesser nature.[64] I think we are right to say that the idea of a total hierarchical structure for the totality of all existing realities on an important point is broken and contradicted.

Thus what we find in the theology of Gregory is a structure of three, and only three, levels, divine, spiritual and material, or in other terms, God in the proper sense and the two created kinds of nature.

13. The dialectic character of the system

The next thing to which attention should be drawn is to what might be called the *dialectic* character of the system of Gregory. By this is understood a structure or a pattern which both includes (a) an idea of different natures or elements talked about as contrasted and even understood as separate and at a distance from each other, and (b) a bringing together of the same natures and elements.

What we are here confronted with is a kind of basic structure in the thinking of Gregory which we find used and applied more or less all through his system.

This pattern, which means an understanding of, a) different kinds of natures, and b) a bringing together of these natures, is something which we have already met in the anthropology and Christology of Gregory. *In man*, the two kinds of created natures, *spiritual and material*, were brought together, and *in Christ*, the new blending, we have met a further bringing together of God and man, and *created and uncreated*.[65] We have even seen that Christ for Gregory meant a union of *God and matter*. The two elements or natures in the thinking of Gregory that are on the greatest distance from each other and are the two most sharply contrasted.

To this we may add as a last "step", the earlier discussed idea from the *Fourth Theological Oration* about a *final bringing of all by Christ to God*.[66] We may even include the bringing of the body by the soul to God as a feature of this structure.

We have on some occasions noticed that Gregory understood the different natures as being at a kind of distance to each other.[67] We may say that this indicates a feature in his theology of thinking in terms of separateness, as well as union.

14. The dialectic structure as differing from the Platonic tradition

We have thus found that a kind of dialectic scheme is a characteristic feature in the theology and thinking of Gregory. Finally at this point I wish to raise the question about the relation to the Platonic or Platonizing tradition in this respect. A more thorough discussion or investigation of this quesiton would go beyond the limits of this study, but I want though to raise the question and formulate the thesis that we here, in this dialectical structure, find a place where Gregory breaks with the Platonic tradition.

To begin with what regards the understanding of man, the idea of man as a joining or connection between something spiritual and something material might be understood as something in common between Gregory and the Platonic tradition. But, on the other hand, that which regards his understanding of what happens in the incarnation and the resurrection of man as well as the idea of a bringing of all, even the material nature, to God, must be clearly understood to break with this tradition. The very idea of a union or bringing together of the Deity and something material, as I understand it, must be regarded as adverse to and in conflict with one of the basic ideas of the Platonic tradition, the distance between matter and the highest sphere and reality.

A typical feature of the Platonic tradition as already mentioned is the hierarchical scheme or structure. If we now applied this scheme consequently to Christ, he would rather be regarded as an intermediary Being between the highest Godness or Deity and the created world. Now this is not Gregory's Christology. T. Spidlík comments on this and appropriately says that Christ was a mediator not while he was between God and man but because of being both God and man.[68]

So, without having made any thorough study of the issue, my impression is that Gregory with his dialectical pattern differs from the Platonic tradition for which the hierarchical structure is the very characteristic one. Perhaps we may say that the same basic idea, that of different levels of reality, is used in two different ways. In the one case, as an assumption for a consequently realized hierarchical structure, in the other as a base for a dialectic pattern (or rather a combination of a dialectical and a hierarchical structure).

15. A direction "from" God and a direction "back" to God

The third structure which I think we are able to discern in the system of Gregory is a pattern or a scheme which means a kind of direction or "movement" from God and a direction or a "movement" back to God in the creation and the final theosis and restoration. This structure is less dominant or distinctive than the others discussed so far, but this scheme is especially noticeable in the anthropology, and also to a certain extent even in the wider understanding of Gregory as it concerns the relation of the created world to God.

It should even be said that when we talk about a "movement" from God in the creation this must not be literally understood in terms of an emanation or a going out from God, in the sense of an outflow of the divinity itself.

16. Man

When Gregory talks about man and his soul we have seen that he uses expressions which give the idea of a divine origin of man. The soul is talked about as coming from God and divine, it is an inbreathing of God and is even at some occasions talked about as a part of God.[69] In Or. 14.7, Gregory can speak about us as "being a part of God and springing from above."[70] Thus, the texts give a strong impression of a divine origin of man, though Gregory certainly not should be understood as thinking of any heavenly pre-existence of man.[71] As a composed being, we have further understood man as placed at a distance from God, and here we find a kind of direction away from God.

17. The created world

What concerns the creation or the created world as such there are some different factors which I think contribute to the impression of the structure or scheme discussed here.

First, the emanative language should be mentioned, which Gregory uses in the fourth dogmatic poem on the world, describing the coming into existence of the creation. (What concerns the created world as such this kind of emanative language is not found elsewhere in the texts, though Gregory sometimes uses it for the angels.)[72] Thus Gregory, in this poem in the verses following the passage quoted in the beginning of this chapter says that, "Nous brought forth ($\dot{\omega}\delta\acute{\iota}\nu\epsilon\iota\nu$)[73] all".[74]

Further for myself, the two-step character of the creating act even contributes to the impression of a movement from God in the act of creation. As discussed above in some texts, we have found Gregory using a kind of two-step structure in his description of the coming into existence of the world, consisting of, a) a conceiving or initiating of the world, and b) the actual performance or fulfilling of the creative act. Further we have noticed that this kind of talking puts an emphasis on the origin of creation as being within God himself.

Reading what Gregory here is saying, I "visualize" it as a kind of two-step structure which includes an initiating of the creation within God himself, and a placing or putting of the created world at a distance from God (though Gregory generally does not use such a vocabulary),[75] thus starting a kind of "movement" away from God.

In the fourth dogmatic poem, we find such a scheme. We here very clearly find the two-step structure with the initiating of the creation within God, and the later "bringing forth" of it. Gregory here even talks about a presence[76] of the world with God before its coming forth or coming into existence. In this poem, Gregory even talks further on about Logos who "threw" the creation away from God.[77]

So we may here observe a kind of movement or direction away from God in the act of creation. This concerns man as we have understood him as being placed at a distance from God as a mixed and composed being. This distance further might be understood as the "starting point" for his way to God and the final theosis.

This way to God even includes the bringing of the body, a part of the material creation, to God. If creation might thus be understood as implying a kind of direction from God, the final theosis of man means a kind of movement towards God and a direction toward him which affects both kinds of created natures (the material and the spiritual) in the figure and shape of man.

To some extent, as it concerns the creation as such, I even think we are able to go one step further. In one of the theological orations we have met the idea of a final bringing of all to God, when God will be all in all.[78] This idea as we have seen is not any further developed in the texts, but here we find a hint of an idea of a final bringing of all to God. Systematically speaking, here lies a movement "back"to God of the created reality.

Thus, I think that we find very clearly in the way of man the scheme or structure discussed here, and to a certain extent even to that which concerns the creation as such.

Chapter 5
Man and Trinity

1. Introduction

There is a strong love for the divine in the writings of Gregory and we have noted a certain attractiveness to this.[1] The divine for Gregory is the holy Trinity or Triad and much of his theology is occupied with the theology of the Triune God and a defence of the proper understanding of its nature and inner relations. So Gregory in Or. 16.9 talks about the resurrection and the heavenly life when "some will be received by the unutterable light and the contemplation of the holy and royal Trinity, enlightening more clear and pure and wholly mingling Itself with the whole mind, in which solely and beyond else I hold the kingdom of heaven to exist."

In this chapter, some different aspects of the relation of the Trinity to man and to creation shall be discussed.

In the thinking of Gregory, the second of the divine Hypostases, the Son or the Mind or Word of God, has a strong position as the creating agent as well as the incarnate God and as Saviour. I here wish to show that even the other two of the divine Hypostases or Persons (the Father as well as the Spirit in a certain number of texts) are talked about as having a kind of role in the act of creation or a relation to the world. This is also useful as otherwise we risk an overly Christocentric understanding of the thinking of Gregory.

Further, what I want to discuss here is the relation of God to creation as such rather than the saving work by God for man and creation in need of salvation and restoration. Thus rather what might be called the economy of creation than the economy of salvation.

2. A differentiation within the act of creation

In Or. 38.9 when Gregory talks about the creation of the angels he says that God, or rather "the Good", when he wanted to multiply the objects for his goodness "conceived ($\dot{\varepsilon}\nu\nu o\varepsilon\tilde{\imath}\nu$) the angelic and heavenly powers. And this conception ($\dot{\varepsilon}\nu\nu\dot{o}\eta\mu a$) was a work fulfilled ($\sigma\nu\mu\pi\lambda\eta\rho o\tilde{\nu}\nu$) by the Word and perfected (completed, $\tau\varepsilon\lambda\varepsilon\iota o\tilde{\nu}\nu$) by the Spirit."[2]

In the fourth theological oration in a similar way we find Gregory expressing the role of the Father and the Son respectively in the creation of the world. He here is saying, "Is it not clear that of the same actions the Father intimates the models (ἐνσημαίνεσθαι) and the Word brings them to pass (ἐπιτελεῖν)."

What we here come upon is a kind of differentiation of the role of the divine Persons in the act of creation and we shall in this section examine this differentiation. Differentiating in such a way is now more clear in regard to the role of the two first Persons, the Father and the Son or the Word of God. As to what a specific role is assigned to the Spirit already in the creation, the text quoted above is without any direct parallel. It is clear though that Gregory, on the whole, regarded the Spirit as the perfecting agent. With this text as a basis though we shall discuss and show a possible way of understanding or interpreting Gregory.

3. The Father and the Son

The Son of God, or the Word or Mind of God, has a strong position as creating agent in the writings of Gregory. He is the Creator Word.[3] Further, he is not only spoken of as the one by which the world is made or by whom God has made it[4] but even more strongly spoken of as Creator (δημιουργός)[5] and as creating.[6]

Now this strong position could be misunderstood if we don't understand it against the background of the relation of the Son or the Word to the Father or to God as such as it concerns the creative action.

Here some sayings of Gregory are of interest. In some texts we especially find him making the kind of differentiation previously referred to with regard to the role of the Father and the Son in the act of creating. In attempting to formulate this we may say that the Father or, as in Or. 38.9, God as such is understood as the initiating one, whereas the Son is understood as the one who does the actual creating.

In Or. 30.11 in the context of the close relationship of the Son to the Father, Gregory talks about the creation of the world and states that the Father impresses (ἐνσημαίνεσθαι) the models of the same actions, and the Word brings them to pass. Further, in order to stress the unity of the Father and the Son, Gregory says that the Son is doing this like the Father (πατρικῶς). In PD 8. 55–56 we find Gregory talking about Logos who created the world "following the design of the great Father". So we may do some systematizing of the sayings of Gregory in some texts[7] and talk about the Father as initiating the creation and the Son as the performing one.

When Gregory more directly talks about the second Person as creating I think we often should have the sayings discussed above as a background. In the preceding chapter on the theological system of Gregory, we have noticed the variety of terms which Gregory is using when he talks about creating and the creating act.[8] Of these terms I would understand those with the meaning of "cause to exist", "become" or "be given existence to" etc.[9] to have the more precisely qualified meaning. When Gregory speaks now about the Son or the Word of God as Creator and as creating it is possible to notice that he is generally not using these qualified terms but others (δημιουργεῖν, πηγνύναι, τεύχειν).[10] The terms which I understand as more qualified are generally assigned to God as such.[11] In translating the terms used for the creating activity of the Word, it should perhaps therefore be understood with the emphasis of performing the creation or establishing the world.[12]

In the dogmatic poems, especially the fourth on the creation of the world, the role of the Mind as creating or world-establishing and engendering is strongly emphasized.[13] Even here I think the sayings should be understood though against the background of what has been said above. In the beginning of the fourth poem Gregory thus states that the forms "became" when the great God wanted it.[14] Further on in the poem the role of the divine concept (νόησις) and Mind as world engendering is strongly emphasized.[15] Here I think we even are right to keep in mind the sayings of Gregory in the first dogmatic poem on the Father when he talks about the Son as "founder of the world" (κοσμοθέτης), "The Father's might and conception (νόημα)".[16]

In the preceding chapter we have observed a kind of two-step character of the creating act consisting of, on the one hand the conceiving or initiating of the world in the thoughts of God, and on the other hand, the actual performance of the creation. It should here be stated that these two steps not totally correspond to the activity of the Father and the Son respectively as discussed in this paragraph, at least not what concerns the understanding of Gregory in his fourth dogmatic poem on the creation, where the Son or the Mind of God as his "conception" must already be said to be involved in the "first step", the conceiving by God of the world.

4. The Spirit

In the preceding section we have discussed the strong position of the second divine Person as creating agent and emphasized the necessity of the fact that this position should be understood towards the background of the relation of the Son or the Mind of God to the Father or to God as such. We have even discussed a number of texts in which we find Gregory making a kind of differentiation of that which concerns the roles of the Father and the Son respectively as initiating and performing the act of creation.

In Or. 38.9, we also find a special "role" or function assigned to the Spirit, which in the act of creating or coming into existence of the angels is talked about as perfecting or completing this work. What we here come upon is thus a differentiation in the act of creation which even includes the Spirit and we shall in this section discuss such a relation of the Spirit to the creation and the created world.

In great parts of the Christian tradition the work and acting of the Holy Spirit is understood as related to the so called economy of salvation, that is, the work of God on man in need of salvation. Now, what we find here in one text of Gregory is an attribution of a function to the Spirit already in the act of creation or, systematically speaking, what might be called the economy of creation. Now this is not a very frequent idea in the thinking of Gregory and we find it in a passage which concerns the creation of the angels and not the world or creation as such. I nevertheless think it is worth noticing, and further I want to show a possible way of interpreting Gregory which concerns an understanding of an applying of such a function of the Spirit on man.

In Or. 38.9 (a passage which is without any direct parallel[17]), we find the Spirit talked about as having a function in the act of creation. In some other texts we find the Spirit talked about as having a relation to the created world. In Or. 39.12 Gregory for example makes a relation of the created world to the three divine Persons as those "of", "through" and "in" (ἐκ, διὰ, ἐν) everything is, whereas in Or. 34.15 the Spirit is referred to as the one "through" (διὰ) which all is.

I have wanted to mention these texts to show that even the Spirit is thus understood as having a relation to the creation and the created world as such, expressed in different ways in different texts.[18]

A certain parallel to the formula of Or. 38.9 is found in Or. 34.8. Here the Father, the Son and the Holy Spirit are talked about as Cause, Creator and Perfecter, (αἴτιον, δημιουργός, τελειοποιοῦν). This saying is without any direct relation to the creation or any object as such and I suppose that here on the whole Gregory is thinking about the Spirit as "perfecter" without any explicit relating of this to the creation or the work of the salvation and sanctification of man. It is clear though that Gregory, as expressed in this text, on the whole, regarded the Holy Spirit as "perfecting". So he, in Or. 41.11, says about the angels, "For from nowhere else comes their perfection and illumination and their difficulty or impossibility to move towards evil than from the holy Spirit", and in some other texts (which rather should be referred to the economy of salvation)[19] the Spirit is spoken of as "perfecting".

5. An interpretation of the Spirit as perfecting

I so want to show a possible way of interpreting Gregory which concerns an application to man of what has been said above about the Spirit and its function. It should clearly be said and stated that this interpretation is made by the author out of some of the ideas of Gregory, or with the thinking of Gregory as a base and thus not is an interpretation discussed or expressed by Gregory himself.

That which now makes this interpretation possible are two facts. 1) The fact that the original, primal man for Gregory was an immature being. 2) And further the fact that Gregory on the whole regarded perfection as related to the Holy Spirit.

As has been discussed in a previous chapter, Gregory understood Adam, the first man, as an immature being, and different aspects of this primal "infancy" have been discussed. Adam was still immature and we have understood him as described with a certain weakness and ambiguity. Further, he was endowed with a free will and should by himself acquire the good and the life with God. Combining these ideas or this set of ideas about the primal man, it is also possible to interpret the thinking of Gregory as implying the understanding of an original growth or progress of man, though he himself does not speak directly in such terms.

The original man may thus be spoken of with a formulation which is not Gregory's own, as not yet perfect. This now gives us a particular opportunity to interpret and understand what has been said above about the Spirit as having a relation not only to salvation, but even to the creation as such and about the Spirit as the perfecting one. If man from the beginning was still not yet perfect we may understand his perfecting by the Spirit as something waiting ahead and not yet fulfilled. In Or. 38.9 Gregory talks about the creation of the angels using the three step formula discussed above consisting of, causing — creating — completing/perfecting. If we now compare this to the creation of man, we may make an interpretation which understands man as a being whose perfection by the Spirit (even in the primal state before any fall of man) was not yet fulfilled in the creation but waiting and a question of future.

If we even take the idea of a growth or progress of man into consideration, which we above have seen as a possibility in interpreting Gregory, we may, in summary, formulate a possible interpretation or further-interpretation of the ideas of Gregory as following.

Man from the beginning was an immature being whose perfection and fulfilment still was waiting ahead. He was free on his own to choose the good and acquire that for which he longed. Now, we may understand the Spirit as the "perfecting one", and as especially related to this effort and growth or progress of man. Further, the earthly life of man, at a distance from God, may be said to be the scene of this growth and effort of man whose "teleiosis", perfection and fulfilment still was waiting ahead of him. And so we here find a kind of original significance of the life on earth of man and a corresponding function of the Holy Spirit.[20]

6. The position of the Father

In the teaching of Gregory on the Triune God, the Father has a strong position as source and principle for the other two Persons.[21] From the Father the Son is begotten and from the Father the Spirit is proceeding.[22]

Concerning the relationship of God to creation I think we may now talk about a kind of corresponding position and rank of the Father as first principle, at least to a certain degree taking into regard what has been said above about the Father as initiating the creation.

We have earlier observed and discussed a structure in the "system" of Gregory consisting of a movement or direction from God, and movement back to God in regard to man and the creation. Following the sayings of Gregory discussed above concerning the roles of the Father and the Son in the act of creation, the Father may now be said to be the "starting point" of this movement.

Here further a text should be mentioned where we find an idea, never developed by Gregory in any other text. It concerns an ultimate bringing in the time of restitution of the creation to God and a subjection of all by the Son to the Father. This text is found in Or. 30.5 where Gregory talks about the time of restitution when "all" shall be subjected to Christ and the Son subjects it to the Father or to God.[23] Now we perhaps are bound to talk about a certain balancing of this idea in the text. Gregory here says that "The Son subjects [all] to the Father, and the Father subjects [it] to the Son, the one by his work, the other by his benevolence".

The Father's subjection of all to the Son now might be understood as aiming either at a subjection of all by the Father to the Son in the work of redemption and transformation by Christ, or at an "eternal", "mutual" subjecting which in the latter case means a kind of balancing of the position of the Father. So Gregory further on (Or. 30.6) talks about Christ as all and in all. He here returns to the time of restitution when "God shall be all in all" but repudiates an understanding of this which should mean a "resolving" of the Son into the Father. "God shall be all in all in the time of restitution. Not in the sense that the Father alone will be and the Son wholly resolved into Him ... but the whole of God, when we shall be no longer divided as now by movements and passions and containing nothing at all of God in ourselves or very little, but [when we on the contrary shall be] wholly like God and able to contain the whole of God and only God. For this is the perfection (alt. consummation, τελείωσις) to which we hasten." And so Gregory at last talks about Christ as "all and in all". Here we may talk about the Father as the ultimate goal, even for the movement "back" of the creation.

Much of the interest in the writings of Gregory concerns the true nature of the Triune God and the understanding of the relationships of the Son and the Spirit to the Father. Here the Father, himself "ἄναρχος"[24], without source, is understood as principle and cause for the two others; the Son who is begotten of him and the Spirit who is proceeding from him.[25] Among the sayings of Gregory there are some few passages and formulations which give the impression that Gregory seems to regard this relations as a kind of movement or progress expressed by dynamic terms. I here want to mention these formulations and show the possibility to understand them as expressing on the one hand a kind of movement from the Father within the Trinity as such, and on the other hand, with a more or less certainty, even a kind of movement "back" to the Father.

In one of the theological orations Gregory states thus, "Therefore the monad from the beginning moving to duality came to rest in the triad. And this is for us the Father and the Son and the holy Spirit."[26]

A certain parallel is found in Or. 23.8, which is quoted further down in the text. What we here find is an expression of a movement from the Father in the Trinity. In Or. 42.15, we find a passage which is possible to read as an expression of a movement from the Father as well as back to the Father. "The Union is the Father from whom and to whom the others are brought in order". (For the Greek text and for an alternative reading and translation not denoting a movement see note nr. 27.)

I want to mention these passages, for along with the reading of them as expressing a movement from the Father within the Trinity as well as a movement back to the Father, we here find a parallel to one of the structures discussed in the preceding chapter. We there observed a structure of the "system" of Gregory consisting of a kind of movement or direction from God in the act of creation as well as a movement or direction back to God. What we here may thus notice is a parallel between a dynamic understanding of the inner-Trinitarian life and the relation of man and even to some extent of creation as such to God.

We have earlier discussed composition and the composite character of man, as well as the fact that this is for Gregory related to sin. We have even talked about it as involving a risk of inner opposition and separation.[28] In commenting upon this we may say that composition for Gregory has an unsatisfying aspect or side. Finally here should one passage concerning the Trinity be mentioned which I find of interest. Here it may be said that Gregory is expressing the idea that the Triad or Trinity transcends or is above duality. "A perfect Triad of three perfect ones, a Monad moved because of its richness. But the Duad is surpassed—for [the Triad] is above matter and form of which the bodies consist—. A Triad defined through its perfection, for as the first it goes beyond the composition of duality, in order that the Divinity neither may remain scanty nor be shed out boundless."[29]

Notes

Chapter 1

[1] The Trinitarian theology of Gregory of Nazianzus is the object of J. Hergenröthe⟂,
Die Lehre von der göttlichen Dreieinigkeit nach dem heiligen Gregor von Nazianz,
Regensburg 1850. The study by C. Ullmann, *Gregorius von Nazianz der Theologe,*
Darmstad 1825, deals with the most of his theology, including his teaching on the
Trinity and Christ.

There is, to my knowledge, no modern study on the Trinitarian theology of
Gregory though his Christology is the object of F. Norris, *Gregory of Nazianzen's
Doctrine of Jesus Christ,* Ph.D. Dissertation, Yale University, 1970. Diss. Abst. nr.
71–17.015.

[2] For Basil see M. Orphanos, *Creation and Salvation according to St. Basil of
Caesarea,* Athens 1975.

Among the works on Gregory of Nyssa which might be mentioned are:
Gaith, J., *La conception de la liberté chez Grégoire de Nysse,* Paris 1953
Ladner, G., "The Philosophical Anthropology of Saint Gregory of Nyssa", *DOP*
12, 1958
Leys, R., *L'Image de Dieu chez Saint Grégoire de Nysse,* Brussels and Paris 1951
*Κ. ΣΚΟΥΤΕΡΗ, ΣΥΝΕΠΕΙΑΙ ΤΗΣ ΠΤΩΣΕΩΣ ΚΑΙ ΛΟΥΤΡΟΝ
ΠΑΛΙΓΓΕΝΕΣΙΑΣ. ('Εκ τῆς ἀνθρωπολογίας τοῦ ἁγίου Γρηγορίου Νύσσης).
ΑΘΗΝΑΙ* 1973 (C. Scouteris, *Consequences of the Fall and the Laver of Regenera-
tion. From the Anthropology of St. Gregory of Nyssa.* Athens 1973.)

[3] In a very good article, B. Otis makes an attempt to understand the Cappadocian
theology towards the background of the whole fourth century and the different
theological streams current then. Though in many details I disagree with the author,
I appreciate his grasp of the issue, which is worthy of being followed up in more extended studies.
B. Otis, "Cappadocian Thought as a Coherent System", *DOP* 12, 1958

[4] The dialectical system of Gregory discussed in chapter 4 in this study might be seen
as a foreshadowing of the theological system of Maximus. (As a matter of fact,
Maximus is said to do some commenting upon Gregory in his writings.) For the
theology of Maximus, see L. Thunberg, *Microcosm and Mediator,* Lund 1965.

[5] For a definition of the use of the term in this study see Chapter 1.4 and especially
Chapter 2.1.

[6] See Orphanos p. 81. Gregory of Nyssa thus does not distinguish between an
"image" of God given to man in creation and a "likeness" which man himself
should acquire. (See further ch. 2.5.d). I think though that the "likeness" given
already in the creation not should be understood in a static way in the thinking of
Gregory of Nyssa and thus even in his case one should reckon with some kind of
progress of man.

[7] In the writings of Irenaeus, we meet the famous idea about the original "infancy" of
Adam. The first man, Adam, as a newly created being was not yet perfect (*Ap.* 12

and 14). It is now possible to question if this idea had any special function in the theology of Irenaeus and, if so, what function?

To my understanding it is possible to understand the function of this idea as following, reconstructing it out of the sayings of Irenaeus. In the confrontations with the Gnostics, Irenaeus was forced to work with the question of evil and its origin. Against the Gnostics he with the Christian tradition had to claim that the body as well as matter as such was good and that evil could not accordingly be derivated from these natures. But from where did evil then originate and what was its cause? Irenaeus now seems to be forced to derive it from God himself. Against this idea he gives the answer that the fault is not God's but the opposite, man's (*Adv. Haer.* 4.39.3, 4.39.1, cf. 4.38.4). There has been a fall of sin, a lapse and a transgression. The cause is thus man, who was created as a free being with a power over himself (*Ap.* 11, *Adv. Haer.* 4.38.4, 4.39.3).

But, if man from the beginning was a good and perfect being, how could he then commit sin and suffer a fall? Here we now find the idea about the infancy of Adam. He was thus from the beginning not perfect and could easily suffer a fall and be easily led astray (*Ap.* 12, *Adv. Haer.* 4.38.1). So the idea about the original infancy of Adam helps Irenaeus to answer the question about evil. Here even the idea about the original freedom of man has a function. Thus the idea about the infancy of man, as well as his freedom, has the function of answering the question about the origin of evil and the possibility of a fall. Here we also find the idea of the persuasion by Satan. This idea, together with the idea about the fall of Satan, becomes a kind of intermediary link in the explanation of evil (*Ap.* 12 and 16).

(*Ap.* = The Apostolic Preaching, in English translation: St. Irenaeus, *The Demonstration of the Apostolic Preaching*, J.A. Robinson, London 1920.
Adv. Haer. = Adversus Haereses, in English translation: Irenaeus, Against Heresies, in *The Ante-Nicene Fathers*, Vol. 1, Michigan 1950.)

[8] Cf. note nr. 5.

[9] Cf. H. Koch, *Pronoia und Paideusis*, Berlin und Leipzig, 1932.

[10] See for example, chapter 16, in Gregory of Nyssa, "On the making of Man", in the English edition in *A Select Library of the Nicene and Post-Nicene Fathers*, Vol 5, Michigan 1954.

[11] Here when "Platonism" is talked about, or the Platonic or Platonizing tradition, the whole Platonizing or the Plato-expounding tradition is being considered from Plato himself, over middle Platonism, to Plotinus and so-called "neo-Platonism". This is of course a highly fluid tradition, which along its way even absorbs elements from other philosophic schools, especially Stoicism. Arnou, in his very informative article about the Platonism of the Fathers, "Platonism des Pères", talks about "un platonisme en marche" (*DTC* 12, col. 2259).

Within this whole, long, and fluid tradition there are, in spite of all the differences between the different "systems" or sketches of systems found within it, certain common and typical features. For example, the dualistic view on man given account for in the text above following this note. Some other typical features of it will be discussed particularly in the fourth chapter on the "system" of Gregory.
Literature:
R. Arnou, article "Platonisme des Pères", *DTC* 12, 1935
A. Armstrong, *An Introduction to Ancient Philosophy*, London 1947.
F. Coplestone, *A History of Philosophy*, Vol. 1, Norwich 1946.
E. v. Ivánka, *Plato Christianus*, Einsiedeln 1964.

[12] H. Pinault, *Le Platonisme de saint Grégoire de Nazianze*, La Roche-sur-Yon 1925.
E. Fleury, *Hellénisme et christianisme: Saint Grégoire de Nazianze et son temps*, Paris 1930.
(This study is by P. Gallay, in his book about the life of Gregory, characterized as more literary than historic, p. XIV.)
J. Plagnieux, *Saint Grégoire de Nazianze théologien*, Paris 1951, Chapitre Premier. See also R. Ruether, *Gregory of Nazianzus, Rhetor and Philosopher*, Oxford-London 1969.

[13] See for example Fleury, pp. 21, 72, 156, Pinault pp. 1, 5, 13, 57, 243, Plagnieux pp. 27, 33.

[14] See for example the presentation and mentioning of J. Draeseke, A. Harnack and others in Pinault p. 2 f.

[15] Ruether p. 15.

[16] Or. 7.23.

[17] See ch. 3.2.

[18] See ch. 3.5 (point 4.b) and ch. 7.b.

[19] Lengthy lists of literature on Gregory are given especially in H. Althaus, *Die Heilslehre des heiligen Gregor von Nazianz*, Münster 1972, J. Mossay, *La mort et l'au-delà dans s. Grégoire de Nazianze,* Louvain 1966.
See also P. Gallay, *La vie de saint Grégoire de Nazianze*, Lyon-Paris, 1943.

[20] Cf. note nr. 1.
See also J. Plagnieux, *Saint Grégoire de Nazianze théologien*, Paris 1951,
Δ. ΤΣΑΜΗ, ΔΙΑΛΑΚΤΙΚΗ ΦΥΣΙΣ ΤΗΣ ΔΙΔΑΣΚΑΛΙΑΣ ΓΡΗΓΟΡΙΟΥ ΤΟΥ ΘΕΟΛΟΓΟΥ, ΘΕΣΣΑΛΟΝΙΚΗ 1969. (T. Tsami, *The Dialectical Character of the Teaching of Gregory the Theologian*, with English summary.)
B. Otis, "Cappadocian Thought as a Coherent System", *DOP* 12, 1958.

[21] See also J. Szymusiak, *L'homme et sa destinée selon Grégoire le Théologien*, Thèse, Paris 1958, *Eléments de théologie de l'homme selon s. Grégoire de Nazianze*, Roma, Pontificia Universitas Gregoriana 1963, and "Grégoire de Nazianze et le péché", in Studia Patristica 9, *TU* 94, Berlin 1966.
D. Winslow, *The Concept of Salvation in the Writings of Gregory of Nazianzus*, Thesis, Harvard University, Cambridge, Massachusetts, 1967.
See also the article by B. Otis mentioned under note 20, F. Hümmer, *Des hl. Gregor von Nazianz, des Theologen, Lehre von der Gnade*, Kempten 1890 and C. Ullmann, *Gregorius von Nazianz der Theologe*, Darmstadt 1825.

[22] Portmann, p. 68.

[23] Portmann, p. 78.

[24] In the so called Benedictine edition found in the patristic serie of Migne, *PG* nr. 35 and 36.

[25] Found in *PG* nr. 37, col. 398 f., Carmina, Liber I, Poemata Theologica, Sectio I, Poemata Dogmatica 1—38. (In some literature referred to as Carmen 1.1.1—38.) Here referred to as *PD* 1—38.

[26] *PG*, nr. 37, col. 175, 193 and 392.
Also published in a critical edition in *Sources Chrétiennes*.

[27] F. Lefherz, *Studien zu Gregor von Nazianz*, Bonn 1958, p. 67. Here also some inauthentic additions to some of the orations are mentioned. Lefherz here goes back to a work published by T. Sinko, and my study also owes a debt to the writings of Sinko. Concerning the forementioned additions, on one occasion Sinko seems to take a positive view toward the authenticity of the passage referred to. I use this passage with reference to Sinko's work (Ch. 2.6.g, note nr. 125). T. Sinko, *De traditione orationum Gregorii Nazianzeni*. Pars Prima. Meletemata patristica 2, Cracoviae 1917, pp. 168—176.

[28] Lefherz, p. 68f.

[29] For the different editions, for the critical textual work completed up to now, questions of authenticity, etc. see F. Lefherz, *Studien zu Gregor von Nazianz, Mythologien, Überlieferung, Scholiasten,* Bonn 1958, T. Sinko, *De traditione orationum Gregorii Nazianzeni.* Pars prima et secunda, Cracoviae 1917 and 1923, in Meletemata patristica 2 and 3.
D. Meehan, "Editions of Saint Gregory of Nazianzus", *Irish Theological Quarterly,* 18, 1951 and the introductions to the different modern critical editions.
See also in P. Gallay, *La Vie de Saint Grégoire de Nazianze,* Lyon - Paris 1943, p. IX f. for the oldest editions of the work of Gregory.

Chapter 2

[1] This term is used to denote that Gregory regarded man as a kind of double or composed being, made up by two natures or components, body and soul, or matter and spirit.

[2] Or. 40.8.

[3] Or. 2.75.

[4] *PD* 8.70f., cf. Or. 38.11.

[5] Or. 38.11, cf. *PD* 8.1 and 8.80f.

[6] Or. 2.75, 7.23, 14.7 and 38.11.

[7] Or. 7.23.

[8] Or. 2.74, 7.19, 17.4, 18.3. Cf. Or. 18.42.

[9] Or. 2.74, 7.23 and 18.42.

[10] Or. 7.19 and 18.3.

[11] See also *The Dogmatic Poems*, especially nr 4 and 8.

[12] Or. 38.7.

[13] Or. 7.22.

[14] Or. 40.5. Cf. Or. 38.11 and 6.12.

[15] Or. 40.5.

[16] Cf. ch. 4.17.

[17] Or. 6.22 and 28.3. This is probably even the meaning of *PD* 4.84ff. For a discussion of this text see ch. 3.2.

[18] Or. 28.31. Cf. Or. 44.3.

[19] Or. 38.9, *PD* 7.53f, Or. 28.31 and 40.7.

[20] Or. 28.31 and 38.9. See further ch. 3.6.h.

[21] *PD* 7.23f.

[22] Or. 38.11. Cf. Or. 40.5.

[23] Or. 40.5.

[24] Or. 28.12 and 38.11.

[25] Cf. ch. 2.6.g and note 124.

[26] Or. 2.17–18, 18.3, 7.21 and 38.9.

[27] Or. 7.23, 38.9 and 40.2.

[28] *PD* 8.1f. Cf. *PD* 8.70f and 4.91. See also Or. 38.11.

[29] Cf. Or. 40.2.

[30] Cf. Or. 2.28.

[31] A three-partite division ($\sigma\tilde{\omega}\mu\alpha$, $\psi\upsilon\chi\dot{\eta}$, $\nuο\tilde{\upsilon}\varsigma$, the terminology is not quite consistent): Or. 32.9, *PD* 10.2.
A four-partite division ($\sigma\tilde{\omega}\mu\alpha$, $\psi\upsilon\chi\dot{\eta}$, $\lambda\acute{o}\gamma\varsigma$) Ep. 101, col. 184, Ep. 102, col. 196.

[32] *PD* 8.1f.

[33] Cf. note 28 above.

[34] *PD* 8.72f. " Ἐν γὰρ ἕηκε πνεῦμα, τὸ δὴ θεότητος ἀειδέος ἐστὶν ἀπορρώξ."

[35] Or. 14.7. "μοῖρα Θεοῦ, καὶ ἄνωθεν ῥεύσαντες".

[36] Cf. Or. 7.19.

[37] Or. 38.11.

[38] Or. 2.17, 7.21 and 16.15.

[39] Or. 7.20 and 7.23.

[40] Or. 2.22, 7.21 and 28.28.

[41] Or. 21.1–2.

[42] Or. 2.22.

[43] Of these terms, $\lambda\omega\gamma\iota\kappa\acute{o}\varsigma$ has a more limited, rational meaning.
$Nο\varepsilon\rho\acute{o}\varsigma$, Or. 38.11, *PD* 4.77. cf. Or 21.1 and *PD* 8.66.
$\Lambda ο\gamma\iota\kappa\acute{o}\varsigma$, Or. 12.1, 28.13, 30.20 and 32.9.

[44] Or. 21.1–2 and 38.11.

[45] See note 31 above.

[46] $\Lambda\acute{o}\gamma ο\varsigma$, Or. 16.15, 21.2 and 28.16.
$\Delta\iota\acute{\alpha}\nu ο\iota\alpha$, Or. 7.21, 28.11 and 28.28.

[47] Or. 39.7. Cf. Or. 8.9 and 45.3.

[48] Or. 7.21, 16.15, 28.28 and 37.11. See also Or. 21.2.

100

[49] Cf. Or. 21.1.

[50] Or. 2.74, 12.4, 18.4, 21.2, 27.10, 28.2, 39.9, and 40.46.

[51] Or. 39.8. Cf. Or. 38.7 and 2.7.

[52] Or. 34.12. Cf. Or. 17.9 and 32.27.

[53] Or. 38.7, 39.7, 39.10 and 40.5.

[54] *PD* 8.80f. Cf. Or. 38.11.

[55] Or. 28.17.

[56] For this distinction see for example, L. Thunberg, *Microcosm and Mediator*, p. 127 ff. Concerning the three Cappadocian theologians, M.A. Orphanos states that Basil made this distinction whereas Gregory of Nyssa did not. M.A. Orphanos, *Creation and Salvation according to St. Basil of Caesarea*, p. 80 f. For Gregory of Nyssa see though note nr. 6, ch. 1.

[57] Or. 30.6, 38.7, 39.10, 40.5 and 40.8. In Or. 24.10 and 28.17 we find though another use of the term.

[58] Or. 8.6, 24.15, 32.15. In Or. 6.14 the therm ὁμοίωσις is used. So in Or. 39.7, he even speaks about us who were made for "μίμησις", imitation of God.

[59] Or. 1.4, 2.22 and 6.14.

[60] Cf. Or. 30.20 and 38.13.

[61] Or. 1.4.

[62] Or. 17.9, 24.15, 33.12 and 37.22.

[63] Or. 1.4, 16.15. Cf. Or. 33.12.

[64] Cf. Or. 8.10.

[65] Or. 7.23.

[66] Or. 8.23, 12.4 and 16.9.

[67] Θέωσις, Or. 17.9 and 21.1.
Θεὸς γίγνεσθαι, Or. 7.23, 29.19 and 30.21.
Θεοῦν, Or. 34.12, 38.11 and 40.42.
Θεοποιεῖν, Or. 2.22, 30.14 and 31.4.

[68] Or. 30.4 and 40.6.

[69] Winslow, who regards *theosis* as an important notion in the thinking of Gregory, has a chapter on this theme in his study. He here talks both about what *theosis* is and what it is not, and describing it talks about "a dynamic relationship between man and God" (p. 172). He even talks about the fluidity of the term and states "that any attempt to understand what Gregory means by *theosis* must take into account the fluidity both of the term itself as well as his use of it, avoiding any attempt to arrive at a fixed definition." (p. 175). D. Winslow, *The Concept of Salvation in the Writings of Gregory of Nazianzus*, p. 154 ff.

[70] Or. 38.13, Ep. 101, for example col. 177, 184 and 188.

[71] Cf. Or. 40.5–10.

[72] Or. 31.4.

[73] Or. 29.19. Cf. *PD* 11.9.

[74] Or. 30.14. Cf. Or. 30.21. For the significance for man of the incarnation see also Or. 7.23, 30.6, 38.13 and 45.22.

[75] Note though Or. 31.4. See also Or. 38.7.

[76] See note 50 above.

[77] *PD* 8.72 f.

[78] See ch. 2.1.

[79] Or. 2.17–18, 27.7 and 30.20.

[80] Or. 28.12.

[81] Or. 7.22.

[82] Ch. 2.6.h.

[83] Or. 38.10.

[84] Or. 28.6, 28.22–30. Cf. Or. 38.11.

[85] *PD* 8.67. Cf. Or. 16.5.

[86] Ch. 2.6.g.

[87] Chf. 2.1.

[88] Or. 7.19. See also Or. 7.20–23 and 18.3.

[89] Cf. Or. 2.81, 6.16, 16.17, 19.14 and *PD* 8.112–118. See also Or. 38.12.

[90] Cf. Or. 21.25 and 30.5.

[91] Or. 14.6–7.

[92] Or. 7.20 and 7.23.

[93] Or. 2.18, 27.7 and 30.20.

[94] Or. 39.7. Cf. note 47 above.

[95] Or. 2.91.

[96] Or. 2.17, 2.74, 28.4, 28.12, 38.12–13 and *PD* 10.3.

[97] Cf. Or. 2.74 and 28.4.

[98] Or. 21.2 and 39.8. See also Or. 17.4, 28.12 and 32.15.

[99] Or. 28.12.

[100] Or. 7.21, 18.4. Cf. Or. 16.15.

[101] Or. 18.4. See also Or. 38.7–8 and 21.1–2.

[102] Or. 2.7. See also Or. 28.11–13.

[103] Or. 28.11–13.

[104] A passage in Or. 19.14 hardly seems to contribute to the solution of the question, "Ταῦτα τὸ ξύλον, καὶ ἡ πικρὰ γεῦσις ... Ἐντεῦθεν γυμνὸς ἐγὼ καὶ ἀσχήμων, καὶ τὴν γύμνωσιν ἔγνων, καὶ τὸν δερμάτινον χιτῶνα ἡμμιασάμην, - - ".

[105] Ch. 3.2.

[106] An idea as a matter of fact expressed in Or. 38.11–12, the text just discussed.

[107] Or. 38.13.

[108] Or. 14.6.

[109] Cf. Or. 7.21.

[110] Cf. Or. 2.17 and 7.21.

[111] Or. 7.21 and 7.23.

[112] "καὶ γενομένη σὺν τούτῳ ἓν καὶ πνεῦμα, καὶ νοῦς, καὶ θεός, - - ".

[113] Or. 7.21.

[114] Or. 7.21.

[115] Or. 7.23.

[116] Or. 7.21. "ἓν καὶ πνεῦμα, καὶ νοῦς, καὶ Θεός".

[117] Or. 7.21. "ὅλον εἰς ἑαυτὴν ἀναλώσασα".

[118] Or 7.21.

[119] Or. 2.17.

[120] Or. 30.20.

[121] Or. 2.76.

[122] Or. 28.8.

[123] Cf. Or. 28.5 ff.

[124] Or. 38.10.

[125] Or. 6.22, 28.3, 31.15, 40.7, *PD* 4.84–92 (for a discussion of this text and an alternative reading of it, see ch. 3.2) and *PD* 7.53–55. See also Or. 34.8 and Or. 44.4. Sinko who discusses the last passage should probably be understood to regard it as authentic, T. Sinko, p. 170 f. (Cf. note 27, ch. 1.)

[126] See further ch. 4.9.

[127] Or. 30.21. Cf. Or. 30.13 and 38.14.

[128] Ch. 2.6.b and 2.6.f.

[129] Or. 21.25.

[130] Or. 7.21.

[131] Or. 30.4–6. For a further discussion of this text, see ch. 5.6.

[132] See ch. 2.6.a and 2.6.b.

[133] Ch. 1.2 and esp. ch. 2.1.

[134] Ch. 2.1.

[135] Cf. Or. 38.10, 28.6 and 28.26 ff.

[136] Or. 18.3, 7.22 and 7.19.

137 See ch. 2.6.b.

138 Cf. ch. 2.6.b and some of the main texts presented in ch. 3.2.

139 For Plato, see Armstrong, p. 49 f.
For Plotinos, see Armstrong, p. 194 and Coplestone, p. 469.

140 For his understanding of the creation of matter as well as the forms, see *PD* 4.3 ff.

141 Cf. ch. 2.1.

142 Or. 7.23.

143 *PD* 8.81, Or. 2.17, 38.11 and 28.22. *PD* 4.92, Or. 2.75, 40.7 and 28.3. See also Or. 2.18, 14.7 and 18.3.

144 Κρᾶμα, Or. 14.7, 27.7, 28.3 and 38.11.
Μίξις, Or. 28.22 and 38.11.
Portmann gives an account for the Stoic background of the terms κρᾶσις and μίξις and states that Gregory is using them without making any differentiation between them. Portmann thus seems to understand the two terms κρᾶμα and κρᾶσις as equal. The latter is not found in any of the passages referred to above, though it is used in the Christology (Or. 38.13, cf. Or. 34,10, ἀνάκρασις). Portmann, p. 64.

145 "ζῶον ἕν ἐξ ἀμφοτέρων," Or. 38.11, cf. Or. 2.75 and *PD* 8.65.

146 "τὸν αὐτὸν, πνεῦμα καὶ σάρκα", cf. Or. 14.7.

147 Portmann, p. 68 ff.

148 Portmann, p. 68.

149 See also ch. 3.3 and 3.7.c. This motif, as well as its background in general ancient thinking, is discussed at length by Portmann (p. 63 ff.), as well as by Spidlik (p. 83 ff.).

150 Note though Or. 28.22.

151 Or. 38.11.

152 *PD* 8.61–73.

153 Portmann, pp. 63 and 65 f.

154 Or. 38.11. Cf. Or. 14.23.

155 In this passage Gregory does not refer to the compound of man but is rather making a statement as such.

156 "Σύνθεσις γὰρ ἀρχὴ μάχης, μαχὴ δὲ διαστάσεως, ἡ δὲ λύσεως." Or. 28.7.

157 "Σύνθεσις γὰρ ἀρχὴ διαστάσεως."

158 Cf. Or. 31.15.

159 Cf. ch. 2.6.d.

160 Which is the case in the death of man. Or. 7.21 and 38.11.

161 Ch. 2.6.f.

162 Cf. also Or. 28.22, where Gregory asking talks about "our first moulding and composition (σύστασις)" and "our last formation (μόρφωσις) and completion (τελείωσις)".

Chapter 3

[1] Or. 14.7. Cf. Or. 2.17.

[2] Cf. Or. 14.2.

[3] Cf. Or. 16.15, see also Or. 7.21.

[4] Or. 28.11.

[5] See note 26.

[6] Cf. Or. 32.15, see also Or. 14.33.

[7] "... therefore the high Logos, being kindly minded, threw the mortal nature away from the angelic troops, so much light now surrounding the throne..." With this translation it is shown that only man (and not the angels) is understood to be "thrown away" from God.

[8] *PD* 4.46 f. Cf. *PD* 7.56 f.

[9] Ch. 2.6.g and ch. 2, note 125.

[10] More or less directly expressed in Or. 38.10 and the text discussed here, or presupposed in others of the passages referred to in note 125, ch. 2.

[11] Γαῖα δ' ἔτι ζώοισιν ἀγάλλεται ἀφραδέεσσι, cf. Or. 39.13.

[12] Cf. Or. 39.13.

[13] Or. 38.12, *PD* 8.111 and *PD* 9.82f. See also Or. 39.7 and the discussion in ch. 2.5.d.

[14] Or. 28.12 and 38.11.

[15] Or. 38.12. Cf. Or. 2.25 and 39.7.

[16] In *PD* 8.107 f. the tree though is understood as concerning a judgment of good and evil.

[17] Cf. Or. 2.25 and 39.7. In these texts the tree of knowledge is said to be partaken of "not in due time and improperly". The tree is though not directly understood as "theoria".

[18] Cf. Or. 38.11.

[19] Cf. the discussion in ch. 2.6.e.

[20] Or. 28.12.

[21] Or. 28.12.

[22] *PD* 9.86.

[23] Or. 14.7, 28.12, 38.11 and *PD* 4.84 ff, and *PD* 10.19.

[24] *PD* 4.84 f.

[25] Cf. Or. 36.5.

[26] Ἔπαρσις has a double meaning of elevation and elation or pride.
Althaus on p. 55 and in note 58, pleads against Sinko for the latter meaning of this term in Or. 38.11, "Erhebung". Further evidence for this translation is found in Or. 38.9 and 36.5 (both cases concern Lucifer) and in *PD* 10.19 concerning man. See also Or. 14.7.
In Or. 28.12 I have chosen though the translation, "elevation" for the term ἔπαρσις.

[27] *PD* 4.46.

[28] Or. 38.9

[29] Or. 28.12. See also *PD* 4.46 and *PD* 10.56 f.

[30] Cf. Or. 28.12.

[31] Or. 28.12 and *PD* 4.84 f. For a discussion of the latter text, see above ch. 3.2.

[32] Or. 28.12 and 38.11–12.

[33] *PD* 4.84 f. Cf. note 31 above.

[34] Or. 38.12. Cf. Or. 2.25 and 39.7, for these passages see the commentary in note 17 above.

[35] Or. 38.12.

[36] Or. 2.23–24.

[37] Or. 38.12, 45.28. See also Or. 2.17.

[38] Or. 2.17, cf. Or. 38.12, see ch. 3.2., text nr. 1.

[39] Or. 2.15.

[40] Cf. Or. 31.25.

[41] Or. 37.16 and 37.20.

[42] Althaus, pp. 56, 80 f., 88 and 93.

[43] Althaus, pp. 81 and 92 f.

[44] Althaus, p. 92.

[45] Althaus, p. 92.

[46] Althaus, pp. 81 and 93.

[47] Cf. ch. 3.6.e.

[48] See further ch. 3.6.1.

[49] Cf. Althaus p. 55.

[50] Or. 2.23–24. Cf. Or. 38.12.

[51] Or. 2.23. See also Or. 39.7.

[52] Cf. the discussion of this passage in ch. 2.7.c.

[53] Cf. Or. 16.15 and *PD* 7.53 f.

[54] Σύνθεσις γὰρ ἀρχὴ μάχης· μαχὴ δὲ διαστάσεως· ἡ δὲ λύσεως· See also Or. 31.15.

[55] Or. 28.31, 38.9 and *PD* 7.53 f. See also Or. 31.15.

[56] Or. 38.9.

[57] Or. 28.31 and 38.9.

[58] Perhaps Or. 31.15 might be read like that. In PD 7.15 ff. and *PD* 7.52 f. the angels are talked about as non-material but yet with the possibility of sinning.

[59] This is the way Althaus understands him in the short run. Only the body of man is

the place and origin of the passions (p. 23 ff.), or with a tripartite division of man, the body and the lower part of the soul (p. 28 f.). Further, Althaus does not understand the higher rational and spiritual part of man, "der Geist", as being able of going against God willingly. It is thus rather dubiously understood as a "captive" (pp. 41 and 81). I am doubtful as to the legitimacy of this systematizing of the thinking of Gregory. Are there really no spiritual passions? What about the pride, and what about the self-elevation? Probably Or. 37.22 might be read like this, where we find Gregory exhorting, "Cut off the bodily passions (σωματικός), cut off also the spiritual (ψυχικός)."

[60] The passage is found in ch. 3.5.

[61] Or. 2.17.

[62] Or. 16.15 and *PD* 7.52 f.

[63] Cf. Althaus p. 91.

[64] Or. 37.15.

[65] Althaus pp. 56, 88 and 93.

[66] Althaus p. 22 ff.

[67] Althaus pp. 22 ff, 41 and 81. Cf. the discussion in note 59 above.

[68] Althaus pp. 41 and 81.

[69] Althaus pp. 79 f. and 92 f.

[70] Althaus pp. 70 and 89 f. See also p. 60.

[71] Cf. ch. 3.6.f.

[72] Althaus p. 89 f.

[73] Althaus p. 91.

[74] Ch. 3.6.i.

[75] Otis, p. 102 f.

[76] Cf. De Principiis, 1.6.2 and 2.9.2 and 2.9.6, *The Ante-Nicene Fathers*, Vol. 4, Michigan 1951, and H. Koch, *Pronoia und Paideusis*, p. 105 f.

[77] See Contra Celsum, 6.44, Origen, *Contra Celsum*, translated by H. Chadwick, Cambridge 1953. See also H. Koch, p. 107. Koch regards though the idea of free will as the main aspect.

[78] Which I personally wish to question. Otis p. 102.

[79] Otis, pp. 103 and 110.

[80] Otis, p. 102.

[81] Otis, pp. 102 and 115 f.

[82] Otis, p. 114 f. See also p. 108 f.

[83] Otis, p. 108 ff. I think Otis is quite right in what he says about Cappadocian mysticism, nevertheless in one of our texts above, Or. 28,12, there is something similar to the idea of "satiation".

[84] Ch. 3.6.h.

[85] Otis, p. 110.

[86] G. Ladner, The Philosophical Anthropology of Saint Gregory of Nyssa, *DOP* 12, 1958, p. 93, note 152.

[87] Otis, pp. 109, 116 and 122.

[88] Otis, p. 112, note 39. Basil, *PG* 29.13B. For this idea, found in the writings of Basil, see Orphanos, p. 62 f.

[89] Portmann, pp. 71 and 77—79.

[90] Portmann, p. 77, cf. p. 69.

[91] Spidlík, pp. 79—80.

[92] Plagnieux, pp. 425—428.

[93] Winslow, p. 54. A similar attitude is found in *TΣAMH*, "Man, of his own free will and through the weakness of his intellect, allowed himself to be led astray by Satan's power of persuasion. (In the English summary, p. 182.)

[94] Or. 28.12.

[95] *PD* 4.84 f.

[96] See ch. 2.6.g. and note 125, ch. 2.

[97] *PD* 4.84 f. Cf. ch. 3.2, the comment on text no. 5.

[98] Or. 2.17.

[99] Ch. 3.6.i.

[100] *PD* 4.84 f, Or. 28.12 and perhaps even Or. 14.7.

[101] The idea of a "divine paidagogia" of man is especially observed by F. Portmann in his study, *Die göttliche Paidagogia bei Gregor von Nazianz*. See for example p. 73.

[102] Althaus stresses the relation between the body and its sufferings and the correction of man, and regards the body as a necessary condition for the salvation of man. Man is, according to Althaus, created as "erlösungsfähig", that is "capable of being saved", p. 56 f.

[103] Or. 2.17, 28.12. Cf. Or. 38.12. See also Or. 14.6.

[104] Or. 2.17.

[105] Or. 2.17, cf. Or. 38.12.

[106] Or. 2.17, cf. Or. 28.12.

[107] Althaus, p. 60 f. Portmann, pp. 71 and 84.

[108] Althaus, pp. 61 and 90.

[109] Portmann, p. 71.

[110] Or. 2.17.

[111] Althaus, p. 61.

[112] Portmann, p. 25. Cf. pp. 60 and 84 f. See also Althaus p. 68 f.

[113] Ch. 3.6.f.

[114] Ch. 3.6.i.

[115] Ch. 3.5.

[116] Cf. *PD* 8.101 f. and 9.82 f.

[117] See ch. 2.7.b.

[118] See Spidlík p. 104 ff. and Thunberg p. 140 ff.

[119] Or. 2.17 and 16.15. See also Or. 7.21 and 14.2.

[120] See *PD* 8.57, the alternative reading of the text given above, ch. 3.2, text number 6. Cf. Or. 39.13.

Chapter 4

[1] See further the distinction between God and creation, ch. 4.3.

[2] Cf. Althaus, p. 45.

[3] Cf. *PD* 4.83.

[4] Cf. the reference to God's own self-contemplation in Or. 38.9 and 40.5.

[5] Althaus, p. 46.

[6] Ποιεῖν, Or. 30.20, 34.8 and 42.8.
Κτίζειν Or. 20.9 and 39.13.
Πηγνύναι, a term used in the dogmatic poems for the world-creating or world-establishing activity of the Mind. See further ch. 5.3, *PD* 4.59, 5.1, 8.55 and 10.2.
Τεύχειν *PD* 5.4 and 8.97.

[7] Or. 32.10, 38.10, 40.7 and 41.2.

[8] Or. 7.19 and 32.7. *PD* 4.6 and 4.20.

[9] Cf. Or. 7.19 and 40.7. See also Or. 19.8 and 38.3.

[10] Or. 30.18, 38.3, 38.7 and 38.13. See also Or. 18.42.

[11] Or. 38.7 and 42.17. See also Or. 6.22.

[12] Or. 18.42 and 38.7.

[13] Cf. Ep 101, col. 181.

[14] *PD* 4.3–6.

[15] Ch. 5.2 and 5.4.

[16] *PD* 4.20 f. and 4.59–76.

[17] Cf. Or. 30.11.

[18] Ch. 4.17.

[19] Or. 38.9–10. Cf. *PD* 8.55 ff.

[20] Ch. 2.3 and note 17, ch. 2.

[21] Ch. 2.6.g and note 125, ch. 2.

[22] Ch. 2.6.g. See also notes 120–122, ch. 2.

[23] See also Or. 28.3 and 41.12.

[24] Ch. 2.7.c.

[25] Ch. 2.2.

[26] Ch. 2.7.b. Cf. also ch. 3.3, point 3.

[27] Ch. 2.5.a.

[28] Or. 14.7.

[29] Cf. *PD* 8.72 f.

[30] Ch. 2.6.f.

[31] Ch. 2.7.c.

[32] Or. 2.17 and 16.15. See also Or. 7.22.

[33] Cf. Or. 7.23. See also Or. 38.13 and ch. 2.5.e.

[34] Or. 31.4, 34.12 and 41.9. See also Or. 31.28 and 40.42.

[35] Or. 2.23 and 38.13. See also Or. 34.10.

[36] For the Christology of Gregory see F. Norris, *Gregory of Nazianzen's Doctrine of Jesus Christ*, Ph.D. Dissertation, Yale University 1970, Diss. Abst. No. 71—17,015.
J. Hergenröther, *Die Lehre von der göttlichen Dreieinigkeit nach dem heiligen Gregor von Nazianz, dem Theologen, mit Berücksichtigung der älteren und neueren Darstellungen dieses Dogmas*, Regensburg 1850, and C. Ullmann, *Gregorius von Nazianz, der Theologe*, Darmstadt 1825.

[37] Or. 29,17, Ep. 101, col. 177—178 and on the whole, Or. 29—30.

[38] Ep. 101, col. 182 f., Ep. 102, col. 196.

[39] Ep. 101, col. 180, Ep. 102, col. 196 and Or. 37.2.

[40] Ep. 101, col. 180.

[41] Or. 2.23, 37.2, 38.13 and *PD* 11.9.

[42] Ch. 2.7.a.

[43] Or. 2.23, 34.10, 37.2, 38.13 and Ep. 101, col. 180. See also Or. 29.19 and *PD* 10. 59.

[44] See note 35 above.

[45] See note 41 above.
About man, see Or. 2.75 and *PD* 8.65.
About Christ, see Or. 2.23 and *PD* 10.50.

[46] Cf. the distinction between God, the one who is, and creation that becomes, ch. 4.3.

[47] Or. 38.2.

[48] Or. 29.18—20, 37.2, 38.1—3, 38.13 and Ep. 101, col. 177 and 180.

[49] Portmann, p. 110.

[50] Ch. 2.1.

[51] Or. 38.11. Cf. Or. 2.75 and 7.23.

[52] Ep. 101, col. 177.

[53] In the case of Plotin, at least some authors observe a kind of nearness of the One to the world, or a kind of presence of it. Armstrong, p. 155, Arnou, col. 2359.

[54] Or. 2.23. Cf. Ep. 101, col. 188 and *PD* 10.56 f.

[55] Ch. 2.4.

[56] See also Or. 30.5—6 and 30.15.

[57] Or. 30.4 and 30.6.

[58] Or. 30.5.

[59] Or. 30.6.

[60] Ch. 2.6.g.

[61] When Spidlík talks about a "universal unificating function" of Christ, this should be understood with some caution. Spidlík, p. 99.

[62] See though note 53 above.

[63] For man, see for example Or. 2.17 and 38.10. See also chap. 3.3, text no. 1. For Christ, see ch. 4.9 above.

[64] See, for example, Or. 2.38, 39.12 and Ep. 101, col. 180.

[65] Portmann, in his commentary on the two "mixings" in man and in Christ, talks about the union of God and created nature in Christ in terms of a bridging of "an infinite gulf" (eine unendliche Kluft).
I think it should be noticed that this latter terminology (an infinite gulf being over-bridged in Christ) belongs rather to the commentary of Portmann upon Gregory than to Gregory himself. Portmann, p. 110.
(Or. 41.12 though might be interpreted according to the understanding of Port-mann.)

[66] See ch. 4.10, ch. 2.6.g and the comment on this text in ch. 5.6.

[67] Ch. 4.5.

[68] Spidlík, p. 100.

[69] See ch. 2.5.a.

[70] Cf. Or. 25.3.

[71] Cf. Or. 37.15.

[72] Or. 40.5 and 45.2.

[73] In J. Mossay, *La mort et l'au-delà dans s. Grégoire de Nazianze*, Louvain 1966, p. 15, there is a reference to L. Méridier, *L'influence de la seconde sophistique sur l'œuvre de Grégoire de Nysse*, Thèse, Paris 1906, p. 100. Méridier here questions whether the term ὠδίνειν still has its meaning. At whatever now this is aimed, in this passage by Gregory it seems most likely that the term ὠδίνειν has the meaning of "bring forth", "give birth".

[74] *PD* 4.75. Cf. *PD* 4.20 f., where it is talked about "θεία νόησις, ἡ πάντων γενέτειρα πολύπλοκος."

[75] See though *PD* 4.87 f.

[76] *PD* 4.67—69. The understanding of Althaus that Gregory here is coming very near the idea of Origen about the eternity of creation might well be questioned. Against this interpretation of the passage speaks the beginning of the poem where Gregory polemizes against the idea that "matter" and "form" should be "σύναρχα", eternal or together with God from the beginning. *PD* 4.3 ff.

[77] *PD* 4.87 ff. For an alternative, though less credible reading of this passage, see ch. 3, note 7.

[78] See ch. 2.6.g and ch. 5.6.

Chapter 5

[1] Ch. 2.5.b.

[2] A certain parallel to the passage is found in Or. 34.8, though without any direct reference to the creation. For a discussion of this text, see ch. 5.4.

[3] Or. 6.14 and 38.11. Cf. *PD* 1.34, κοσμοθέτης and *PD* 4.68, κοσμογόνος νοῦς.

[4] Or. 7.24 and 20.9.

[5] Or. 38.11, ὁ δημιουργός Λόγος and ὁ τεχνίτης Λόγος.

[6] Or. 32.10, 38.11 and *PD* 4.59. See further note 10.

[7] See also *PD* 1.33 f.

[8] Ch. 4.3

[9] See ch. 4.3.

[10] Or. 32.10, 38.11, *PD* 4.59, *PD* 5.1 f. and 5.4, *PD* 8.55 and *PD* 10.1.
In Or. 19.13 we find though an exception to this tendency, cf. Or. 38.3.

[11] Or. 19.8, 38.9, 41.2, 19.8 and *PD* 4.6. See also Or. 32.10.

[12] In the dogmatic poems Gregory is using the term πηγνῦναι (which is not so easy to translate). The Lampe lexicon gives as translation "set up", of creation. (G.W.H. Lampe, *A Patristic Greek Lexicon*[4], Oxford 1976, p. 1080). Perhaps we could use the term world-establishing.

[13] *PD* 1.33 f., 4.20 f., 4.55 ff., 5.1 f., 5.4, 8.55 and 10.1.

[14] *PD* 4.6. He then talks about God as creator (κτίστωρ) (v. 15) and further says that "he thought, and the forms became, the divine conception (νόησις) (v. 20).
Here I think, systematically speaking, we may talk about a foundation of the activity of the divine concept in God as such. The same tendency is noticable in the passage on the act of creation in the verses 55—76.

[15] *PD* 4.55—76.

[16] *PD* 1.33 f. Cf. *PD* 8.55.

[17] A slight parallel is found in Or. 32.10.

[18] For a relation and a function of the Spirit vis-à-vis the created world, see also *PD* 3.6 and Or. 31.29.

[19] Or. 31.6, 31.29. In Or. 40.43 with relation to baptism. See also Or. 40.45.

[20] A hint that Gregory was thinking in terms of progress and perfection is given in Ep. 101 columns 180—181, where he, commenting on Christ, states "Τὸ γὰρ ἠργμένον ἢ προκόπτον ἢ τελειούμενον οὐ Θεός", "For that which has a beginning, or a progress, or is made perfect, is not God."

[21] Or. 30.7 and *PD* 2.21. See also *PD* 2.31.

[22] Or. 30.19 and 39.12.

[23] Cf. 1 Cor. 15:24—28.

[24] Or. 30.7, *PD* 1.31 and *PD* 2.19.

[25] The Father as ἀρχή, Or. 2.38 and *PD* 2.21, as αἰτία, Or. 30.7. Cf. *PD* 2.31 (ῥίζα). γέννησις Or. 30.7. πρόοδος, Or. 2.38.

[26] Or. 29.2. Διὰ τοῦτο μονὰς ἀπ' ἀρχῆς, εἰς δυάδα κινηθεῖσα, μέχρι τριάδος ἔστη. Καὶ τοῦτό ἐστιν ἡμῖν ὁ Πατήρ, καὶ ὁ Υἱός, καὶ τὸ ἅγιον Πνεῦμα.

[27] Or. 42.15. Ἕνωσις δὲ, ὁ Πατὴρ, ἐξ οὗ, καὶ πρὸς ὃν ἀνάγεται τὰ ἑξῆς... With an "abstract" (though perhaps less credible) reading the term ἀνάγεται may be understood as not denoting a movement but a referring of the two others to the Father: "The Union is the Father from which [the others are] and to whom they are referred one after the other."

Cf. Or. 31.14, a passage with a similar ambiguity. Also a passage from *PD* 3.58 ff. should be mentioned, which I understand as aiming at the inner-Trinitarian life. Ὡς εἰς ῥίζαν ἄναρχον ἀνέρχεται [παῖς καὶ Πνεῦμα], οὐ θεότητα Τέμνει ... Ἐκ μονάδος Τριάς ἐστι, καὶ ἐκ Τριάδος μονὰς αὖθις... (v. 58 f. and 60). "To the source without beginning they return, not dividing the Deity ... From the Monad there is a Triad, and from the Triad there is again the Monad."

In these three passages, Or. 29.2, Or. 42.15 and *PD* 3.58 ff., we now find an expression for a movement or reference depending on the reading of the texts. We thus in these texts find an expression for a movement or a reference of the Son and the Spirit to the Father, depending on the reading of the texts.

[28] Ch. 2.7.c. and ch.3.6.h.

[29] Or. 23.8. Cf. Or. 21.2.

Editions

Opera, *PG* 35–37, edition by J.-P. Migne.

Sources Chrétiennes:

— *Discours 1–3*, Paris 1978, ed. J. Bernardi (SCH nr. 247).

— *Discours 20–23*, Paris 1980, ed. J. Mossay (SCH nr. 270).

— *Discours 27–31*, Paris 1978, ed. P. Gallay (SCH nr. 250).

— *Lettres Théologiques*, Paris 1974, ed. P. Gallay (SCH nr. 208), (Letters nr. 101, 102 and 202).

Other writings of St. Gregory that should be mentioned also include editions of his long autobiographical poem, *De Vita Sua*, as well as the critical edition of the rest of his letters:

Gregor von Nazianz, *De Vita Sua*, Heidelberg 1974, ed. C. Jungck (with German translation).

Saint Grégoire de Nazianze, *Lettres 1* and *2*, Paris 1964 and 1967, ed. P. Gallay (with French translation). This edition does not contain the three theological letters.

Translations

Library of the Nicene and Post-Nicene Fathers of the Christian Church, translated into English with prolegomena and explanatory notes. Second series, Vol. 7. Select orations and letters. (Ann Arbor, Michigan 1974, reprinted), pp. 185—498. (C.G. Brown, J.E. Swallow.)

Bibliothek der Kirchenväter, Ausgewählte Schriften des hl. Gregor von Nazianz, Band 1 and 2, Kempten 1874 and 1877.

Bibliothek der Kirchenväter, Des heiligen Bischofs Gregor von Nazianz, Reden, Band 1. Rede 1—20, München 1928.

Gallay, P., *Grégoire de Nazianze, Poèmes et lettres*, Lyon-Paris 1941. (Extracts from the dogmatic poems at pp. 126—138.)

Translations are also found in the editions of *Sources Chrétiennes*.

Literature

Althaus, H., *Die Heilslehre des heiligen Gregor von Nazianz,* Münster 1972.

Armstrong, A., *An Introduction to Ancient Philosophy,* London 1947.

Arnou, R., art. "Platonisme des Pères", *DTC* 12, 1935.

Coplestone, F., *A History of Philosophy, 1. Greece and Rome,* Norwich 1946.

Fleury, E., *Hellénisme et christianisme: Saint Grégorie de Nazianze et son temps,* Paris, 1930.

Gaith, J., *La conception de la liberté chez Grégoire de Nysse;* Paris 1953.

Gallay,P., *Grégoire de Nazianze, Poèmes et lettres, — La vie de Saint Grégoire de Nazianze,* Lyon-Paris 1943.

Hergenröther, J., *Die Lehre von der göttlichen Dreieinigkeit nach dem heiligen Gregor von Nazianz, dem Theologen, mit Berücksichtigung der älteren und neueren Darstellungen dieses Dogmas,* Regensburg, 1850.

Hümmer, F.K., *Des hl. Gregor von Nazianz, des Theologen, Lehre von der Gnade. Eine dogmatisch-patristische Studie,* Kempten 1890.

Ivánka, E. von, *Plato Christianus,* Einsiedeln 1964.

Koch, H., *Pronoia und Paideusis. Studien über Origenes und sein Verhältnis zum Platonismus,* Berlin-Leipzig 1932.

Ladner, G.B., "The Philosophical Anthropology of Saint Gregory of Nyssa", *DOP* 12, 1958.

Lampe, G.W.H., (ed.) *A Patristic Greek Lexicon*[4], Oxford 1976.

Lefherz, F., *Studien zu Gregor von Nazianz. Mythologie, Überlieferung, Scholiasten,* Diss., Bonn 1958.

Leys, R., *L'Image de Dieu chez Saint Grégoire de Nysse,* Brussels and Paris 1951.

Meehan, D., Editions of Saint Gregory of Nazianzus, *Irish Theological Quarterly* 18, 1951.

Méridier, L., *L'influence de la seconde sophistique sur l'œuvre de Grégoire de Nysse,* Thèse, Paris 1906.

Mossay, J., *La mort et l'au-delà dans s. Grégoire de Nazianze,* Louvain 1966.

Norris, F., *Gregory of Nazianzus' Doctrine of Jesus Christ,* Ph.D. Diss., Yale Univ. 1970 (Diss. Abst. No. 71—17.015).

Orphanos, M., *Creation and Salvation according to St. Basil of Caesarea,* Athens 1975.

Otis, B., "Cappadocian Thought as a Coherent System", *DOP* 12, 1958.

Pinault, H., *Le Platonisme de saint Grégoire de Nazianze. Essai sur les relations du christianisme et de l'hellenisme dans son œuvre théologique,* La Roche-sur-Yon 1925.

Plagnieux, J., *Saint Grégoire de Nazianze théologien,* Paris 1951.

Portmann, F.X., *Die göttliche Paidagogia bei Gregor von Nazianz. Eine dogmengeschichtliche Studie,* St. Ottilien 1954.

Ruether, R.R., *Gregory of Nazianzus, Rhetor and Philosopher,* Oxford-London 1969.

Sinko, T., *De traditione orationum Gregorii Nazianzeni.* Pars prima. De traditione directa (Meletemata patristica 2), Cracoviae 1917.

— *De traditione orationum Gregorii Nazianzeni.* Pars secunda. De traditione indirecta (Meletemata patristica 3), Cracoviae 1923.

ΣΚΟΥΤΕΡΗ, Κ.Β., ΣΥΝΕΠΕΙΑΙ ΤΗΣ ΠΤΩΣΕΩΣ ΚΑΙ ΛΟΥΤΡΟΝ ΠΑΛΙΓΓΕΝΕΣΙΑΣ, 'Εκ τῆς ἀνθρωπολογίας τοῦ ἁγίου Γρηγορίου Νύσσης, (C.B. Scouteris, *Consequences of the Fall and the Laver of Regeneration. From the Anthropology of St. Gregory of Nyssa.*) Athens 1973.

Spidlík, Th., *Grégoire de Nazianze. Introduction à l'étude de sa doctrine spirituelle,* Rome 1971.

Szymusiak, J.M., *Éléments de théologie de l'homme selon s. Grégoire de Nazianze,* Roma, Pontificia Universitas Gregoriana 1963.

— "Grégoire de Nazianze et le péché", Studia Patristica 9, *TU* 94, Berlin 1966.

— *L'homme et sa destinée selon Grégoire le Théologien,* Thèse, Paris 1958.

Thunberg, L., *Microcosm and Mediator,* Lund 1965.

ΤΣΑΜΗ, Δ., ΔΙΑΛΕΚΤΙΚΗ ΦΥΣΙΣ ΤΗΣ ΔΙΔΑΣΚΑΛΙΑΣ ΓΡΗΓΟΡΙΟΥ ΤΟΥ ΘΕΟΛΟΓΟΥ (Tsami, D., *The Dialectical Character of the Teaching of Gregory the Theologian*), Thessaloniki 1969.

Ullman, C., *Gregorius von Nazianz der Theologe. Ein Beitrag zur Kirchen- und Dogmengeschichte des vierten Jahrhunderts,* Darmstadt 1825.

Winslow, D., *The Concept of Salvation in the Writings of Gregory Nazianzus*, Thesis, Harvard Univ., Cambridge, Massachusetts, 1967.

Abbreviations

Works of Gregory:

Ep.	Epistula
Or.	Oratio
PD	Poemata Dogmatica

General abbreviations:

col.	column
DOP	*Dumbarton Oaks Papers.* Cambridge (Mass.), 1941 ff.
DTC	*Dictionnaire de Théologie Catholique,* ed. A. Vacant, E. Mangenot and E. Amann. Paris 1903—1950.
PG	Migne, *Patrologia Graeca.*
SCH	*Sources Chrétiennes*, ed. by H. de Lubac, J. Daniélou and C. Mondésert, Paris 1941 ff.
TU	*Texte und Untersuchungen zur Geschichte der altchristlichen Litteratur*, Leipzig and Berlin 1882 ff.

Index of names

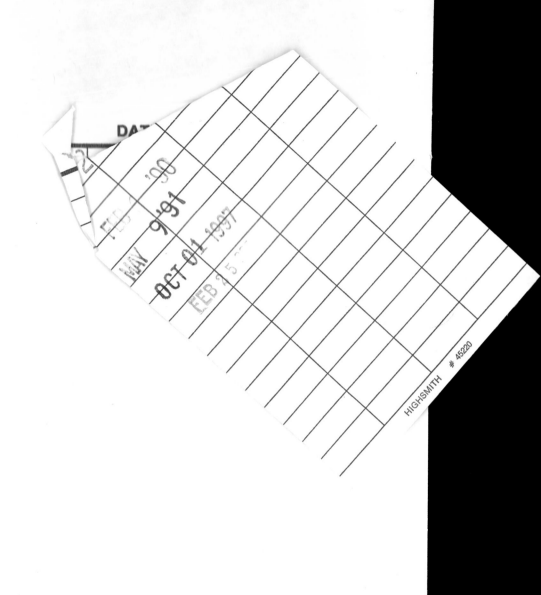